True Tales of a Golden leprechaun

True Tales of a Golden leprechaun

You Won't Believe This, But…!

Graham Van Zant

Copyright © 2024 by Graham Van Zant

All Rights Reserved

No part of this book may be reproduced or transmitted in any form or by any means, electronic or mechanical, including photocopying, recording, or by any information storage and retrieval system without the written permission of the author, except where permitted by law.

*This book is dedicated to my older brother, Don,
who passed on before this book could be published.*

*It has an interesting title but as you read along,
I believe you will see why it was chosen.*

On father's day of 2023 Michael's eldest son wrote this poem as a tribute to his father.

My Dad

I've wanted so much to be like him
And have done all I could to be like him
I've watched him all the years I've grown
And I think of all the baseballs we've thrown

He's shown me how to love God and Christ
And his guidance and love have kept me straight

I so much want to be like him
And there is so much I have because of him

With him are some of the best times I've had
And I'll never forget all the great times we've had

I've loved God and Christ because of him
And I so much want to be like them

Now I have kids of my own
And Oh how quickly they've grown
And I have tried to teach them to be like him
Because more people should want to be like him
Oh how much I love him
He is my Dad and my friend

Michael O'Rilev Jr

Contents

Introduction	I
Michael—The Son, The Brother, The Husband, and Father	1
Michael—The Athlete	31
Michael—The Entrepreneur	49
Michael—The Horse Whisperer	128
Fulfilling A Dream	194
Michael—Man Of God	211
Some Final Thoughts	226

 # Introduction

Do you believe in leprechauns? Until this book was begun, I was not sure I did. To me, they have been part of the fanciful Folklore of the Irish. They were called The Little People. Part of their legend, it has been told, is that they have a hidden pot of gold. They are known to be quite mischievous and enjoy tricking those who might want to steal their gold. Since I have become acquainted with Michael, I am starting to believe they do exist. The main character of this book may possibly be one. During his life, he has escaped the jaws of death more times than any normal human being would care to experience. He has been able to accumulate several pots of good through the many endeavours he has been involved in.

These are his stories as he has told them to me, which makes me wonder. Maybe, by the time you finish reading his tales, you may, as well, start to believe he could be one. This particular and possible leprechaun, known as Michael, although not large in stature, is yet of a size that one could observe to be a slightly overgrown example of such a species. His very mischievous green, twinkling eyes give light to his playful nature when one engages him in conversation.

He loves to tell stories, and you, the reader, are about to embark upon a very interesting journey. The tales he tells of his travels through life are very interesting and entertaining, indeed.

Michael has been around in this particular form for over 79 years. He is quietly spoken, and his favourite expression is, "You may not believe this, but I promise you it is not BS." Hence the subtitle of this book. With this said, we will step forth into the life path of this individual and let you decide whether to believe or not believe in the reality of leprechauns.

It is interesting that this book was almost not completed.

I had spoken with him a couple of weeks before we even began. He had already related to me several of his stories. I told him I would very much like to chronicle his life experiences as they were very entertaining. I felt that many others would, as well, also find them so. We met again a couple of weeks later. I asked him how he was doing. He told me he was very lucky he was still here. Surprised, I asked him what had happened to him. Apparently, a medication he had been taking for some time had caused a very serious allergic reaction. It was to a point where he could barely breathe. This occurred in the middle of the night, at about 3 a.m. He had not been feeling well and was having difficulty breathing. He had dressed himself to go to the hospital but then thought maybe it would pass if he just lay back down for a while.

Things did not improve but continued to worsen. He continued to think maybe he should get up and go to the emergency and get checked out. Michael, in fact, said he heard the voice of God tell him to get up and go to the hospital immediately. Literally, thank God he did. He drove himself to the closest hospital emergency, which, thankfully, was fairly close by. When he entered, the nurse on duty immediately observed his condition and called the doctor on duty, who quickly came out to see him and check out what was happening.

Upon observing his condition, the doctor asked Michael two quick questions. First, have you been taking a particular drug for some time? Secondly, how did you get here? Michael could only nod his head. His whole face was puffed out. His throat, tongue, and lips were so swollen he could barely breathe through his nose. He pointed to himself on the question of who had driven him there. The doctor gasped and said, "That's impossible. The stage you are in, you should be dead by now." He immediately called for two orderlies to grab Michael, and they rushed him right away into an operating room.

Michael was put out and operated on immediately. He told me, "The problem was, I did not go fully unconscious right away." For this operation, his body was fully paralyzed, and he could only move his eyes. Because his eyes were closed, the doctor assumed he was out. "This was truly one of the scariest times of my life as I could see and hear what was going on. I could also feel the pain of forcing a tube down my throat. I could hear them talking and was fully aware of what they were doing to me." He tried to make them aware that he was conscious by moving his eyes. The whole experience brought back painful memories of an earlier time he was put under.

He was much younger and had fought to come out of it. He did not want to be put under again. It was like déjà vu. A few hours later, when Michael came to, the doctor told him he almost didn't pull through the operation. He told him, if he had waited five minutes more, he probably would not have made it. Thankfully, they were able to save his life, and now we can continue his story. It certainly would have been a very short story otherwise. I guess this could be another possible aspect of being a lucky leprechaun.

This, in fact, was just one in a series of escapes with death. There have been many more, as you shall read. Before we get into the life and adventures of this leprechaun, I bring up the earliest time this fellow had his brush with death. When he was about five, a friend of his mother asked if it was okay to take Michael and his older brother Don with her to the local community pool. His mother said yes, so off they went. Not being a swimmer, Michael stayed near the edge of the pool. After he had been in the pool for a time, he decided to climb out from where he was. He swung his right leg up over the side of the pool. Just along the top was a groove a couple of inches wide with an overhanging lip on either side with water running through it. Michaels' foot went down into the groove and was caught up. In trying to free it, he slipped from the side and was now, more or less, hanging upside down in the pool. He was flailing and starting to take on water. Thankfully, his luck was good. His Angels were watching over him. He was rescued with no damage done other than having a bad scare. This was his first escape from death's door. It would be one of many throughout his life to the present time.

Michael first appeared in North America over seventy-nine years ago. It was the north-eastern part of the USA in the state of Connecticut. He was the second in a family of two boys. His birth father and his mother split up while she was still pregnant with him. His biological father's surname was O'Riley. His mother soon remarried to a submariner whose surname was Sartor. The young family migrated to the west coast a short time after Michael was born. The family lived for a few years around the San Francisco area of California. They then moved to San Diego when he was about five. His new father, being a Navy Submariner, was stationed there. His father spent a good deal of the time at sea, so it was his mother who majorly raised the family.

Michael would be 17 before he discovered that the person, whom he now called Dad, was not his biological father. We will go over more on that later in the book. His mother was a fan of the game of baseball. Much of the influence was due to Michael and Don's love of the game. When they lived in the Bay area, she would often take young Michael and his brother to watch a Triple-A game when the home team was in town. Michael really loved the game and, at a very early age, became very much involved in the sport. He knew the names of all the players.

By the time he was ten, he was keeping very meticulous records of their stats. He knew all their batting averages as well as all the other stats of the players on his favourite home team. By the age of five, he was swinging an adult-sized wooden bat. With most swings, he would connect with most of the pitched balls. When they moved to San Diego, he and his older brother, who both loved all sports, those that had a ball associated with it, would go to the local park. It had a ball field. They would practice for hours on end. They both had very competitive spirits. While Michael was trying to catch up to his older brother, his brother was trying to keep ahead of him.

Sports became a very important part of Michael's life and still is to this very day. Michael reminisces on the fact that when he and his brother played two on two, they never lost a game ever. Sounds kind of unbelievable, but it is true! Then again, we might be talking about a leprechaun.

Michael has lived a very full life, and to give each part of it justice, we will break this book down into several major chapters. Each one will give the reader a different aspect of his life. We will highlight many of his accomplishments.

Before we get very far into this book, I believe it is very important that we give Michael's life philosophy by which he has lived and monitored his life's progress. Michael says, "I love sports, and I have always been a very aggressive athlete. When sports did not work out for me, then I would treat everything else I did in my life as if I was playing a sport. Mainly from the viewpoint of baseball. I work at being the best I can be at it. My sports and work adventures have been more than a joy to be part of throughout my life. Baseball, I loved the most of all sports. Throughout my life, the endeavours I became involved in I treated like the game of baseball. Being the batter, I would closely evaluate the pitch that was thrown. I would play it to have an extremely high batting average with as many home runs as I could manage, including having some grand slams."

The first chapter will go through Michael's life as a brother, a son, a husband, and a man of many talents. We will touch on the highs and lows as well as his major adventures. In the second chapter, we will look at Michael the athlete, his love of sports, his involvement, and his accomplishments in many different types of sports. This book could have been about the life of a great baseball player. Unfortunately, circumstances happened that would change the path he was following. In the third section, we will lay out Michael's many exploits as "The Successful Entrepreneur." He has started and created many successful business ventures, each creating a new pot of gold for himself and his family. The fourth chapter will take a very close look at "Michael the Horse Whisperer." For many years, he bred, trained, and raced horses. He then helped to heal hurting horses by using his knowledge and ability. He did this as a very capable Horse Whisperer and as a Horse Chiropractor.

At the age of 35, Michael and his family obtained their first horses. As with everything he has done, he watched and learned, then taught himself the skills to be very successful in the industry. At one point in his life, Michael and his family became the proud owners of over 40 quarter horses.

Michael learned the fine art of breeding, training, showing, and racing. He went on to produce many quality, sought-after horses. If you are a horse enthusiast, you definitely will want to gain Michael's insights in this chapter.

Last but not least area of Michael's life we are going to look at "The Spiritual side of Michael", which has been a driving force throughout most of his life. He has always been a perfectionist. When he takes on a project, Michael stays focused on it until his objective is achieved. We will have an in-depth look at "Michael's Spiritual Journey", how he found God, and how it has changed his life. This has had the most profound effect on Michael and has helped him to get through some very trying times in his life.

Unfortunately, things happen in life that even a leprechaun finds difficult to deal with. Michael's life is one of gratitude, and he never forgets to thank God each morning when he arises and each night before he goes to sleep. That, now having been said, let's take a close look at his life. We will take a close look at the effects he created for himself and for the many people whose lives he touched.

 # Michael—The Son, The Brother, The Husband, and Father

It is strange how circumstances change and influence things before one is even born, that end up having very profound and lasting effects on one's future.

Michael's life is definitely one that fits into that set of circumstances. You will see how that has occurred as we go through the different chapters. As we stated earlier, Michael's mother was first married to a man named O'Riley. She had one son, Don, with him and was pregnant With Michael when they divorced. Later in the book, you will get to see his biological father as Michael meets and gets to know him as an adult.

She ended up marrying another man quite quickly. This would be Michael's father as far as he was concerned. He was told the truth by his mother when he turned seventeen. His older brother Don, by a year and a half, would turn out to be very instrumental in mentoring and influencing Michael in many areas of his life. Don helped him to be the success he was, especially in the restaurant business. When Michael was barely a year and a half old, his mother and her new husband moved from the east coast of

Connecticut to the west coast of California. They lived in the Bay area of San Francisco for a short period, then moved to the San Diego area where Michael would grow up. Michael's new father was a Submariner and would be at sea for lengthy periods. His mother would be a very big influence on his life. His father, in many ways, would be a major influence as well throughout his life, as you will see. Because of their love of baseball, she would often take Michael and Don to the games when the local team was playing home field. As stated earlier, Michael could swing an adult-sized wooden bat when he was barely five. Michael and his older brother both became excellent athletes in their own right, in several different sports. Here is a picture of Michael, right, Don, left and younger sister Christie and younger brother Terry, with their aunt Helen standing behind them. Michael is about eight here.

The two brothers would spend hours together at the local park in the San Diego area practicing, where they would pitch, throw and hit balls until it became second nature to them both. It was here Michael developed and honed his skills as a future ball player. It became very apparent when he started playing in various little leagues. The time spent paid off, he and his brother never lost a game ever when playing two on two. This included baseball, basketball and football. Sounds unbelievable, but it is really no BS. As he grew older, he became interested in another sport, golf. Again, in golf, he and his brother would practice for hours and both became very proficient players. The skills he learned then, he is still teaching others effectively today.

Michael describes himself as a B student in school. Like all things he was involved in, he gave it his best shot. I found out something unusual about Michael when he was telling me about his life. It was something I would never have thought or suspected, knowing him now.

Michael, growing up and until his early twenties, had a major problem with stuttering. This problem only manifested around people he did not know.

This nervous manifestation would show up, especially if he was put in a position of talking in front of others. Michael said, "I used to dread the thought of a teacher asking me to speak in front of a class." This also happened whenever the phone rang because he didn't know who was on the other end of the line. He couldn't even get out a hello. He and Don had their paper route as youngsters. When it came time to collect each month, Michael found it very frustrating to knock on the door to collect money for the paper. Thankfully, his brother was always with him. If Michael couldn't get the words out, Don would smoothly step in before the customer would even notice. His brother Don was the only person in the family who was fully aware of the extent of Michael's difficulty.

This was fortunately handled when he went through a very difficult, special leadership course in his early twenties. He did it in conjunction with the Bob Cummings multilevel vitamin program. From a very young age, Michael's love of the entrepreneurial spirit showed itself. He would be earning money working together with his older brother. He and his brother had a very successful landscaping business. They developed several happy clients in their neighbourhood. They cut their grass, trimmed around their walkways, trimmed their shrubs and hedges, and pulled all the weeds.

His best friend was always his older brother Don. They would spend many hours together working on their skills in various sports they enjoyed. When it had to do with a ball of any kind, they played it.

Michael and his brother had a younger brother, Terry, and a sister, Christie. Michael loved them dearly. There was not as much personal interaction because of their age differences. His sister became a lawyer and then a teacher. Currently, she is managing the Fresno Community Chorus. His younger brother served in the army. He was a very able and proficient surfer. Terry unfortunately died mysteriously at a young age while he was celebrating his birthday in Tijuana, Mexico. He was only in his early 30s. It was a very sad time for Michael and the rest of his family.

For Michael, it has been his older brother Don that he has been closest to. They both had a very high interest in sports from a young age and worked together on them. When he was about twelve, his father decided to volunteer him in an NRA safety course. A friend of his dad was putting one on. His father obtained for Michael, through a friend in the Marine Corps, a big old ugly orange Marine 22 rifle. It was the size of a full-blown, high-calibre military rifle. You put in 15 bullets through the butt end of the gun. Michael's hand and eye coordination were excellent and proved to be so when it came to shooting. Michael was right-handed but had poor vision in his right eye, so he had to shoot across from his left eye. This was not a barrier to Michael and did not hinder him in his marksmanship. The course on gun safety and marksmanship went on for several weeks. After the course was finished, all the young participants and their families went to a campground in the mountains to have a graduation party. They also had a final shooting contest as part of it. Michael handily won this shoot-off. After it was finished, some of the adults were standing around talking. The class instructor, it appeared, wanted to show his shooting prowess. He took his high-power rifle, a 30-06, and pointed at a big boulder a few hundred yards away. He aimed his rifle at the rock and fired three times. Each time, dust would fly from the rock as the bullet hit it. He then went and set up a soda can in the crutch of a tree about 75 yards away. He once more aimed his heavy rifle. He fired several shots but never hit the can. Michael was watching closely. When the instructor was finished, Michael asked if he could give it a try.

Michael had never fired such a large calibre gun, but the fellow said yes, he could give it a go. He told him it would kick back more than his 22. Michael said he understood and took possession of the heavy rifle.

He sighted it up, fired, and the can went flying. The instructor looked surprised but smiled. Somewhat begrudgingly, congratulated him for such a good shot.

The rest of the adults were very impressed with his accuracy. Michael's confidence in his own ability was never in question. At a very young age, the leprechaun was again demonstrating his abilities and capabilities.

There was another time when Michael and a friend were out on a camping and hunting trip. They were camping up in the mountains and had pitched a tent for the night. They had forgotten the stakes that support ropes could be tied to keep it taut. During the night, it snowed, and the tent collapsed on them. They spent the rest of the night in the cold car, trying to stay warm. The next morning, they continued driving through the mountains. They spot a bird sitting on top of a burned-out tree. They both said. "Let's see who can shoot that bird off the tree." He pulls the car off to the side of the road. His friend is out immediately and getting ready to shoot.

Before his friend can get a shot off, Michael is out of the car. He fires his gun once, and the bird falls out of the tree to the ground. His friend is in disbelief and asks him how he did that. The leprechaun immediately regretted having done so just to prove a point. He vowed never to do anything like that again, and he never did.

Another incident occurred when he was out with a friend who was in the army. He just happened to be a trained marksman. His friend asks Michael if he wants to have a little shooting competition. Michael says sure. They scout around and find an old, discarded Pepsi can. They set it up on a cactus leaf about 50 to 60 feet away. It would barely sit there, but finally, after several attempts, get it to stay precariously on one of the leaves at about eye level. This lightest breeze would have made it fall. They walk back about 50 or more feet and get ready to shoot.

His friend shoots first and misses. Now it is Michael's turn. Piece of cake, he thinks as he lines up. He fires and the can doesn't move. He thinks to himself, "How could I have missed?" His friend shoots again and misses. Michael once more lines up. He takes his time, aims and squeezes the trigger. The can is still sitting there. He thinks to himself, something is wrong here. "Let's go take a look," Michael says. They walk over to the can and look. They see one entry hole in the front, right in the middle. There are two exit holes in the back less than a hair width apart. He has hit it dead center twice in a row and the can hadn't moved. I know it might sound a little hard to believe but it is no BS! Just the leprechaun again? Now, on a completely different subject. Michael's mother liked to play bridge. She had several girlfriends that would get together and play bridge all afternoon.

Sometimes one of the girls could not be there, so there was a hole to fill. His mother had taught him to play bridge. When someone couldn't make it, she would have Michael sit in to fill the hole. This one particular time, it happened to occur when it was a big local tournament.

His mother's partner couldn't make it, so in a pinch, she had Michael fill in. Well, the two almost won the whole darn tournament, coming in a very close second. They were written up in the local paper. Michael became a local celebrity because he was so young and played so well. Michael also learned to play chess quite well. He tells of a story where he and his brother were visiting a friend. He happened to be a professional chess player. He had his own personal library of books on the game of chess. He asks Michael if he wants to play a game. Michael obliges. The fellow checkmates Michael quite quickly with very few moves. This sparks Michael's competitive spirit. He asks Michael if he would like to play another game. Michael, being the person he is, tells him, for sure. This time, he pays much more attention, and the game continues for some time. Michael finally sees a possible opening to checkmate his opponent if he makes one wrong move. Well, his opponent fails to make the correct move, and Michael checkmates him. The look of surprise on the guy's face was priceless. He asks Michael to play another. It was getting late, and his brother saves him, saying, it is time for bed, nighty, night Jim.

Michael completed high school and decided to go to a local college. He was running a local hamburger stand at night and going to college during the day. He was surely burning the candle at both ends. Michael was just 18 but of legal age, so the next occurrence would be logical in his father's eyes. His father had gone out to make his own way at a very young age. He was about 16 when he joined the Navy. He lied about his age and he looked older than 16. Michael and his brother arrive home at about two a.m. in the early morning. Having gone to college all day and worked an evening shift at the hamburger stand, they arrived home very tired. They were shocked when their father opened the front door to greet them. He immediately addresses them and says, "Men, you are going to have to get your gear together and leave tonight. Anything you don't take will be donated to the Salvation Army. "Michael and his brother are quite flabbergasted, to say the least. They had no advance warning that something like this was going to take place. They go into their room to start packing their things. Michael and his brother are very tired and not in the best of moods, to put it mildly. They are in their room for less than half an hour when their father walks to the door to check on their progress.

Michael is not happy and tells him to stay out of their room. His father steps in, and Michael yells at him to get out of the room. His father takes another step and Michael yells at the top of his lungs to get out. To make his point, he kicks the wall and puts his foot through it. His father gets the drift and quickly leaves. Michael says it is the one and only time he ever yelled at his adopted father.

Michael, reflecting on this, thinks this took place because his father had gone out on his own at a very young age himself. He felt it was time for his adopted sons to do the same. It had only been a short time earlier that his mother had told Michael that the father he knew was not his true biological father. Michael had met him on the porch as he came home that evening. He had told him that he knew but still considered him to be his only father. Michael said it was the first and only time he had ever seen his father cry. Michael has said several times that although his adopted father was quite strict with Michael and his brother Don, he still loved him as his father. He was able to appreciate that this fellow had taken on a wife with two sons and raised them as his own. He also said that his father was always liked by anyone who met him. Michael said it was rough at times, kind of like being in boot camp growing up, but he has no regrets about how things went.

They are now out of a place to live. They had to decide what to do and where to go. After all, it is the middle of the night. They decide to go up to Los Angeles. His brother says he can get a job with a fellow he trained for Jack in the Box. Maybe he can get Michael hired- on as well. When they get there, Don is hired, but Michael is not. Michael says not to worry, he will find another one around and get hired, which he does. We will tell that story later. It is another amazing story in itself.

They need a place to stay, so they go driving around the area looking for something. They discover this little rental tucked away amongst the trees down a dark and spooky lane. It happens to be owned by a little old couple in their 90s who have been there since the birth of time, or at least seven decades or so when they were first married.

They have a newer, older house they live in but now rent out the original. The rental is made up of three very tiny buildings for $50 a month. The furthest one down the lane is the bedroom. Michael went back this year to see if it was still there. The only building still standing is the little bedroom. Here below, on the right side, is a picture of it.

Across the path from the bedroom was a tiny doll house kitchen where the ceiling was so low, you had to stoop to not bang your head. Do not forget, we are talking about a slightly oversized leprechaun here. The shower and toilet are in another tiny building thirty yards back down the dark pathway towards the house the old couple resided in. The shower was so small you almost had to keep your elbows on your sides while showering. There always seemed to be a wind blowing in the area. At night, it made spooky sounds as the branches of the trees scraped against the sides of their bedroom. His brother was always thinking that there was someone outside. He would wake Michael up to go take a look. Michael had to keep telling him it was only the wind. This one particular evening, about midnight, Michael arrives home from work before his brother.

It's late, dark, and spooky, with the wind blowing as usual. He parks his car and starts down the path towards the sleeping quarters. He can see the light is on through the tiny window. He thinks to himself, his brother must have left it on when he left in the morning. Every step he takes makes a loud crunching sound as he steps on the dead dried leaves. He gets to the door and, just as he is about to put the Skeleton Key in the lock, I did say Skeleton Key, the light from inside suddenly goes out. Michael is completely spooked. He high tails it back up the trail as fast as he can run, and, he can run fast. He quickly hunkers down behind the old bathroom. He then keeps peering around the corner of the building, back down the path, to see what else might take place. A few minutes later, his brother drives up and parks his car. He gets out and heads down towards the sleeping quarters. As he comes abreast of the bathhouse, he hears a hiss, "Come here, over here." His brother jumps until he realizes it is Michael.

"What's going on?" he asks as he crouches down beside his brother. Michael quickly fills him in on what has gone on so far. He tells Don he has been watching the bedroom ever since to see who comes out. They both are now peering down the path when suddenly, behind them,

"What's going on boys?"

They both nearly jump out of their skins until they realize it is the old landlady. Michael tells her what has occurred. She goes to her house and fetches a flashlight. She then toddles off toward their room. They cautiously follow at a safe distance, ready to run if anything goes wrong. They figured she is old and has lived her life. They are both young, just getting started. The young leprechaun wasn't taking any chances. The landlady goes up to the door, puts in the skeleton key, walks in, looks around, and then comes back out. She says, "Let me go check the breaker."

She goes around the side of the building and the light suddenly comes on. "Just the breaker," she yells out as she comes back around. They both gave a huge sigh of relief. All that had been missing here was the rumble of thunder and the cry of a wolf off in the distance. Despite the spookiness of the location, they ended up staying there for almost a year. Other than the wind blowing and making the usual eerie sounds, nothing else scary happened.

Here is another story of the luck of a leprechaun. Michael and his new wife Margie had just been married.

They had been going together for a few months and decided to get married. It was now their wedding day. They both were avid hockey fans. The League Championship game was being played that evening. They decided to go see the game. During the reception, he rushed down to the arena to get the tickets and then rushed back home. He had purchased two seats down near ice level so they would be up close to the action.

That night, they headed down to watch the game. Michael drove his new 62 Corvette with a 'Just Married' sign on the trunk. Michael parked the car, and then they headed up the steps to the entrance of the arena. He reached into his jacket pocket to retrieve the tickets. They weren't there. He realized he had left them at home in the other jacket, the one he had worn for their wedding ceremony.

Well, they had come this far, it would take some time to go home to get the tickets. They didn't want to miss any of the game. Michael walks up to the man who was taking the tickets to tell him his sad tale. The ticket taker, an older gentleman, smiled and said he understood. He told Michael he had never heard that particular story before. He told Michael he believed him and that he did have tickets. He takes Michael and Margie into the arena and points to the entrance, going down into the stands. Michael tells the usher the same story. The usher smiles and points to a couple of empty seats down near ice level. She tells Michael to take them as no one has shown up to claim them. Michael thanks her for her kindness, and they head down to the seats. When they get there, he now sees they are the seats he had purchased. A coincidence, or just the luck of the leprechaun?

The next day, they go to Disneyland. While they were on The Pirates of the Caribbean ride, Margie asked him, "You do have the tickets for Las Vegas?" This was to be their next stop on their honeymoon. "Of course I do," Michael tells her. They get to Las Vegas, and Michael realizes he has left those behind too. Thankfully, there were records in their system to verify that the hotel and show tickets were indeed paid for. Was that just another lucky break for the leprechaun?

These things just keep occurring that make you wonder. Before Michael was married, he went and officially changed his last name to O'Riley. His brother Don had that last name because his mother was still married to an O'Riley when he was born. Michael was born after she had married a man whose last name was Sartor. Michael was, therefore, given that last name. When his mother told him the story when he was 17, that the man he knew as his father was not his true biological father, he didn't think very much about it. When he knew that he was to marry, he decided to change it as he wanted the same last name as his brother. It wasn't easy to give up the name Sartor as Michael had loved that name and it had been his name as long as he had known. Michael's first son, Michael, was born on the day of their first anniversary. His wife Margie was just over nine months pregnant when their anniversary arrived. Michael decided to take his wife out to a restaurant called The Top Shelf, an upscale eatery in the area. While they were having dinner, his wife kept moving around uncomfortably. Michael asked her what was going on. She told him it was probably false labour pains. As the evening went on, they were becoming more and more frequent. A voice tells the leprechaun something needs to happen. "We need to go now."

Michael tells her, "Let's go see my mom to see what she says." They cut their dinner short. His mother lived close by, so they were there quickly. When they arrived, his mother took one look and said get her to the hospital now. They immediately went to the hospital and checked her in. An hour later, their first son was born, just a few minutes before midnight.

It was a very wonderful first-anniversary present indeed. His second son, Patrick, was born a year later. What a very lucky leprechaun!

Now, the next story is a mix of good and bad luck, but I guess, luckier than not, as he is still here to tell the tale. It was several close brushes with death. This is a very interesting experience the leprechaun went through when he came close to losing his life three times in less than a half hour. This is a tale of:

THE DARKEST OF TIMES

How could a simple bike ride to visit a friend become, some several, death-defying close calls? You may possibly have a hard time believing this but sometimes the truth is a much stranger story than fiction.

Michael and his wife were living in an apartment just inside El Cajon. Michael decided he needed to do some form of exercise. So, he went and bought himself a new ten-speed bicycle. He had never owned or ridden one before. A couple of days later, one late afternoon, he decides to go for a ride. He decides to visit a friend who lives a few miles away. To get to his friend's place, he has to traverse up a long, winding, and very steep hill. It was a tough hill to climb and his gears kept slipping. Being the first ten-speed bike he had ever owned, he didn't fully have its mechanics down. He persevered and finally made up and on top of the long hill. He arrived at his friend's place late in the afternoon. He visited with his friend for a little longer than he had anticipated. It was starting to get dark outside when it was time to head home. His friend offered to put Michael's bike in his vehicle to give him a ride home. Michael said thank you, but no, he had arrived under his own steam. He would get himself home the same way. He wanted to enjoy the easy ride down the hill as it had been such an effort to ride up it to get there. He heads off, and he soon reaches the top of the long hill. It is now pitch black. There are no streetlights out in this location. The road is only two lanes and there are no shoulders. There is a solid hill on his left and a major drop-off on his right. To top it all off, he is wearing a dark jacket and dark shorts. This is tempting fate. It is not a good scene to be riding in the dark. He does have a headlight on the bike. Michael takes a deep breath and starts his trip down the long hill. The hill is quite winding, so you cannot see the bottom from the top.

Michael prays that no cars appear on the road on his downward plunge. He travels very quickly as he wants to get down as fast as possible. He travels a couple hundred yards and his bike light starts to flicker.

These lights used to operate from a little built-in generator that rubbed against the front tire. He prays this is not an omen of worse things to come.

He arrives at the first bend and headlights from a car behind him show up. He makes the first turn, and, oh no, a car is coming up the hill towards him. His best hope is now that he and the two cars don't meet at the same point on the hill. His flickering light now goes completely out. With his dark clothes, he is almost invisible. It is not a good situation at all to be in. The two cars are getting closer and closer.

Michael speeds up, he has to get down this hill alive! The car behind is coming up on him fast. The car coming up the hill is still somewhat further away. At the last possible second, Michael swings his bike over into the left oncoming cars lane. The downward car from behind whizzes by on his right, missing him by bare inches. Michael immediately veers back into the right-hand lane, and the upcoming car whizzes past him, heading up the hill. Whew, that was a close call, he thinks to himself. Michael wants to wipe the sweat from his brow but dares not let go of the handlebars. By this time, Michael is really barrelling down the hill in the pitch black. He applies the brakes to slow down. Sadly, there is little or no response from the inadequate brakes to slow his downward plunge. He realizes they are nowhere near responsive enough for his current situation.

This is not looking good. *What is the plan now?* He asks himself. Michael makes the last turn on the hill and can now see the bottom about a quarter mile away. At the bottom is a cross street, which joins the off-ramps of the freeway. Across the intersection, on the left, on the other side of the freeway, is a single store with an oversized parking lot. His plan is to go under the freeway, cross the intersection and swerve into the parking lot. He can then circle the building until he slows the bike down enough so his poor brakes can get him safely stopped.

He was halfway down the final stretch when he saw a VW car coming toward the entrance of his planned turn-in. He prays it will not move to keep the entrance clear for him. But no, it slowly starts moving out as he turns in towards the lot, trying to miss the car. Unfortunately, It moved forward. Michael careens off the front and goes flying. He tumbles and rolls and finally comes to a stop. He lays there for some moments, taking stock of his situation. He slowly and painfully gets to his feet. Thankfully, nothing appears to have been broken. He sits himself down on a little wall to get his bearings. In the meantime, the driver of the car rushes over and asks him if he is okay. Just to make clear, this accident was not the fault of the driver, as there was no way she could have seen him coming. Michael tells her he thinks so, nothing broken, just sore and a little banged up. After a couple of minutes, he tells her it is okay for her to leave, he will be okay. Michael now examines the bike. It is bent but somewhat rideable and the rest of the way home is more or less flat.

Michael gets back on the bike and slowly continues to head for home. The light on the bike is non-workable and is just hanging now. He has gone less than fifty yards when he comes to a set of railway tracks that cross the street on an angle. They are more or less at the same level as the pavement, but there is a lower groove on either side of the rail itself. This is normally a busy street, but at the current moment, thank God, there are no cars. Because it was pitch black and the shaky state of the bike, the front wheel went down into the groove along the rail.

The bike comes to a very sudden stop, and over the handlebars, Michael flies and lands on his head. Can things get any worse? Well, he is lying face down, barely conscious, in dark clothes in the middle of a busy street. He could easily get run over. But the Good Lord is looking out for Michael. He is lying there momentarily stunned, trying to gather his wits about him. He realizes his predicament and forces himself to get up to get himself and his bike out of the street. He is no sooner clear than cars are now whizzing by.

With his dark clothes, he would not have been seen and may have easily been run over. His story could have ended. He would just have been another statistic of a cyclist, hit and run over by a car. Thank the Lord that was not the case. The leprechaun was saved by the Lord again. Michael rests for a few minutes to clear his head, then painfully gets back on his almost now dysfunctional bike and continues the final leg towards home.

He has to go very slowly due to the bent condition of his bike. He is just a couple hundred feet away from home when the light finally dislodges from the fork and falls down between the front spokes. He comes to an abrupt stop but, this time does not go over the handlebars. Thank God, the bike could not travel very fast. *That's it, no more,* he decides. He now walks the bike the rest of the way home.

It is amazing in less than half an hour, the leprechaun had escaped with his life, at least three times from the jaws of death, and survived to tell the tale. He gets to the apartment building and puts the bent and broken bike in the hallway. He walks into the apartment, and Margie sees him. Her jaw drops.

"What have you been doing to yourself?" she asks him with great concern. You don't want to know, he replies but tells her of his harrowing tale before heading off to take a shower and rest his sore and weary bones.

The leprechaun had survived more encounters with the physical universe. He is a little worse for wear, but he is still alive to tell the tale. About a week later, Michael takes his damaged bike back to the store and returns with a new model. A few days later, he tells Margie he was going to take a ride about the local area to see how safe it was to go riding. He was almost involved in two more accidents that could have easily been worse than the one from his ride down the hill in the dark. He rides his bike home and tells himself, *that's it*.

They move into a new home shortly and he hangs the bike up in the garage and never rides it again. So much for that form of exercise. What do you think of that? Was he a Lucky leprechaun?

Michael was involved with several close calls In his life. With each one, his story could have ended very abruptly, but the Good Lord seemed to have more for Michael to learn. So, escaped death many more times.

He was working one job when he stepped off some plywood sheets covering the rafters of the roof of a large Safeway store in Colorado.

He was working with a partner and, unbeknownst to him, his partner moved one of the plywood sheets that were, butted up against each other. He did not let Michael know, so when Michael stepped back, he stepped into empty space. Michael fell thirty feet straight down and landed, straddling a large cooling motor. He survived once again. Landing on the cooling motor probably saved his life. He didn't break anything but found for a long time it was almost impossible to sit.

Michael told me that in a couple of seconds, as he was falling through the air, he was sure that he was going to die. He told me he had heard stories of one's whole life flashing before your eyes in a split second. He said that is what happened to him, and it was the scariest time in his life. He really thought the end had come for him, yet the lucky leprechaun made it through it to tell another tale.

There was another time he was working at the San Diego Stadium on a scaffold with several other carpenters. He was fifteen feet above the ground. The boards on the scaffold they were standing on were not secured properly. Without warning, they gave way, and he and several others were suddenly airborne. Michael went over backwards and landed on his backside amongst a bunch of pieces of wood. He survived once again with no broken bones or any major injuries. Unlucky but lucky at the same time, it would seem. It was on the same job several weeks later, he was working in the yard and had to go into the tool shed to retrieve the tools he needed. As he was coming out the door, he didn't see a shovel that somehow had fallen across the entrance. He stepped on it, lost his balance, and went tumbling down two steps onto his knees. He was immediately taken to the hospital to get checked out. His leg became badly swollen and was numb for several days. It did heal up after several days, so he was able to go back to work. There have been other life-threatening situations, but each time, he was able to keep carrying on. Can you believe it? Are you starting to wonder just a little yet? He seems to have more lives than a cat. Someone seemed to be watching out for him. Michael and Margie had two sons through their marriage, Michael and Patrick. They more or less followed in their father's footsteps when Michael got into the horse business. Michael continued his entrepreneurial path throughout his life. You will read much more about that in the chapter, Michael the Entrepreneur.

From the stories he has told me, I have learned several things about Michael. He is very loyal to his word. He is a doer and always works towards perfection in any endeavour that he undertakes. He works to follow the teachings of the Bible in all aspects of his life. He is a great friend to have. He is very forgiving of the mistakes of others, but do not purposely cross or try to hurt him, it will cost you. Don't try to take advantage of a leprechaun. Here is another story to show the luck of this leprechaun. This is a fishing story to outdo all fishing stories. Michael and his family were going on a short vacation. They were driving out through the mountain roads of Utah.

Michael observed a group of people fly fishing in a large pond along the side of the road. Michael asked his sons if they would like to stop and do a little fishing. The response was a quick yes. Michael pulls the car off the road, gets out, and walks up to one of the fishermen who is leaving. He asks him how the fishing has been going. The guy tells him it is okay but not anywhere nearly as good as another spot he knows of. Michael asks him where that might be. The fellow then gives him a very lengthy and detailed explanation of the location, how to get there, and how to best catch the trout once you get to fish it. It is quite some distance to get there and is well off the beaten path. He tells Michael he has to continue down the paved road for several more miles until he comes to a gravel road on the right side of the road. Once off the paved road, he has to go quite a distance down the gravel road until he comes to a series of three lakes. He tells him he has to drive past the first two lakes and continue along to the third lake. He has to drive as far as he is able to. Then, he has to walk down to the end of the third lake a few hundred yards and go around to the third point. Once there, he then needs to walk out from the point into the lake until he is at least knee-deep. Now, he needs to cast out as far as he can. He tells Michael, "You will catch a trout on pretty much every cast."

It is such a detailed and elaborate story that it makes Michael wonder if this is just a good story or if it might be real. He seems sincere, so Michael decides to go for it. He gets back in the camper and explains to his family what he has been told. He asks if they want to take a chance on it. There is definite excitement at the anticipation of the prospect of such good fishing. So off they go to find out if it is true or a bunch of malarky. They drive several miles to where the gravel road heads off to, it seems, to nowhere. Down the rough and dusty road, they bounce. Finally, the first lake comes into view. He drives past the first, past the second, and finally up and up to the third lake, where they stop and park their vehicle.

Michael and his family get out their fishing gear and walk to the third point, a good quarter mile. They finally arrive at the place the fellow had told them to go. Michael is still kind of wondering to himself, are we being put on? But what the heck? We are there now, so let's give it a try. He takes his rod and walks out from the shore till he is a little over, knee-high in the water. He casts out his line. It seems that the moment the first cast hits the water, a fish is on the line. So far, the story holds.

Michael tells his sons Michael Jr and Patrick, let's huddle up. Here is what we are going to do. I am going to cast out three lines. I will give one to each of you and one to myself. We are all going to catch one at the same time. Michael casts out the three lines. He quickly gives one to each of the boys and keeps one for himself. It is almost immediately, all three are reeling in a fish at the same time. In very short order, they have all caught their limit. They have more than enough for several meals. They continue to camp there for a couple of days, where they repeat their limit catch each day.

It had certainly been worth following the tip he had been given. Michael said he was eating trout from morning tonight. He ate so much that he had to give up trout for a time. On their trip home, they stopped to get gas in a small Utah Town. Michael asked the attendant if he liked trout. Not too much, he told Michael, but my grandmother sure does. Michael asks him to come around to the back of the camper, where he opens up an ice chest filled with trout. He asked him if his grandmother might like those. "She sure would," the attendant replied.

"Please take them and give them to her," Michael told him.

"Wow, the young fellow said, she sure is going to be surprised with all these fish." Now there is a fishing tale for you. Do you believe that one? It would certainly seem that luck has been following this leprechaun around.

As I mentioned earlier and mention again in The Horse Whisperer, Michael's sons, Michael Jr. and Patrick, followed in their father's footsteps. It was their initial interest in horses that ended up with Michael and his family obtaining and eventually owning more than forty horses. The horses became a family thing. The two boys and Michael's father helped Michael build two beautiful horse barns. While the boys were in their teens, the whole family became volunteer Park Rangers. They would, on weekends and many times during the week, be patrolling Saguaro Nat Monument Park on horseback. There, they would help hikers and horseman visitors in the park. They also helped to ensure that no damage was done to the park so that its natural beauty was maintained.

Michael learned the art and skill of a farrier, so both of his sons became professional farriers.

After thirty years of marriage, Michael and his wife parted Ways. It had not been Michael's decision to do so. It was a shock to Michael and truly caught him blindside. Michael says it was the work of the devil. He was very saddened by it, but he told me it strengthened his own personal relationship with God.

Michael has been a good father, a good husband, and a good friend to all who dealt with him fairly. He has always been ready to help someone in need. He has very much, to the best of his ability, walked the talk with his faith and beliefs.

Michael is on his way to 80 and is still going forward strong. Between his passion for serving the Lord, running a business, Also developing a series of videos to help golfers with their chipping and putting, he keeps moving forward just like the energizer bunny.

Now, let's have a look at the life of Michael, the athlete.

 # Michael—The Athlete

As stated earlier, Michael was barely five years old when he started swinging a bat. This was not a child's bat but an adult-size wooden bat.

Michael, though smaller in stature, was very strong. He has always had great hand and eye coordination. He found it easy to connect with most of the pitches thrown his way. Michael, early on, had aspirations to become a professional baseball player. When the family moved to the San Diego area, he and his brother Don would spend hours working together at a local park. They would throw, pitch, and bat the ball to where they could do it with their eyes closed. Michael attributes much of his competitiveness and drive to his older brother, Don, who was just a year and a half older. I talked to his brother, Don, as I was writing this book. I asked him what he thought about his younger brother. He told me this, "Pound for pound, he has not known a stronger, more aggressive, and go-after-it kind of player than his younger brother Michael. "Don was over six feet and a very athletic fellow.

The two of them spent hours and hours together at that local park, honing their athletic skills and becoming very proficient in playing the game. They also enjoyed and did very well with other sports, such as football, golf and basketball.

Michael was a keen follower of baseball, and, of course, his team was the local team, the Oakland Oaks. They later moved to Vancouver, Canada, and became known as the Vancouver Mounties. Later, when his family moved to San Diego, his team was still the Mounties. The San Diego Padres were the local hometown team and still are to this day. By the age of ten, he was going to as many games as he could when they were playing in San Diego. Even though it was over 30 miles a round trip to the stadium, he would take the bus to the field to watch the game. He always managed to position himself down the left-field line so he could collect foul balls during batting practice. At ten years old, he collected all the team's baseball cards, and he kept very accurate and particular records of all the tats of the players of his teams.

His favourite player was a pitcher called "Two Gun Gettle." He could pitch equally well both left and right-handed. He was fun to watch as he could match up to either right or left-hand batters.

When he was old enough, he joined the local little league, where he really showed his proficiency in playing the game. He played several positions, but because he had such a strong throwing arm, he played center field his first year. In his second year, he played shortstop and pitcher. That year, he pitched six no-hitters and had a 700+ batting average with seven home runs. At a very young age, Michael was surely showing his prowess as a potential professional athlete. This is certainly not any BS.

Michael told me a very interesting story of where he was once punished for being very competent as an athlete. This happened in the sixth grade. He would arrive about half an hour early to school before class started. There was, usually, a game of four squares being played. You would have a square for each player. The object of the game was to hit the square of another player where he could not catch it and return it to another's square. That player would then be knocked out of the game. The one who stayed in the longest without being put out was the winner. On this one morning, when he joined the game, one of the teachers was playing the game with the students. Now, Michael was very fast and agile, so he would get the ball and quickly get it out to another square. Inadvertently, he knocked the teacher out of the game. He wasn't picking out the teacher in particular. It just happened the teacher's square was close to Michael, and Michael was quick and accurate.

The teacher became frustrated because he was losing to a young student. The game ended a few minutes before classes were to commence. The teacher then called out Michael and told him to come to the classroom. He said he wanted to talk to him before class started. Michael wasn't too sure what it was about, but he followed him into the classroom. When they were in the classroom, the teacher went up behind his desk and produced a black Betsy baseball bat. He then started chasing young Michael all around the room while swinging the bat at him.

Michael was scared but was fast and agile and kept well out of his way. He kept pushing desks and Chairs in front of him to block the teachers' way. This went on for several minutes until the bell rang. The other students started to enter the room. The students were looking around the classroom in disbelief, as all the desks and chairs were scattered in major disarray around the room. This teacher was not through with humiliating Michael. He told Michael he had to come in during recess and lunch hour and write out numbers on the chalkboard, from one to a hundred thousand. It seemed like a million to Michael.

Then he cut a big strip of yellow-coloured paper and taped it to Michael's back. He really had it in for Michael. When he got home, Michael told his mother what had happened. She was furious and went to see the principal the same day. The principal, unfortunately, was a wimp and didn't even call the teacher in. The harassment did stop, and Michael had no further run-ins with this nasty teacher. He did have to write out the numbers. The teacher, in fact, probably should have been fired for his actions. In this day and age, it likely would have been. He certainly was not mature enough to be in the position he held. That was the only real negative experience in the leprechaun's school life. He kept his nose clean, kept his grades up, and continued to excel in his sports. Michael continued his baseball career right up until he was about 16. He always had a 300 or better batting average. If you know baseball, that is where the best hitters are. Michael felt he was on his way to achieving the goal he had set for himself at a very young age. Sadly, at the time, Michael's father wasn't aware of Michael's abilities and dreams. He was away at sea a good deal of the time. He did not have the opportunity to go and watch his son play ball. Michael and his older brother had to go out to work while going to high school. That was how his father had come up the line when he was younger. Michael was not just a very proficient baseball player. Michael loved all sports and was very well-versed in football, basketball and the game of golf. He became an excellent golfer at a young age. Here again, he and his older brother practiced endless hours honing their skills in the sports they loved. Because injuries to his shoulder a few years later made it more or less impossible for Michael to be able to pursue a career in professional baseball.

Michael would take up playing semi-pro baseball after he had finished school and had spent a couple of years in the working world. Michael graduated high school and then started college. He was working a full-time job and going to school. Unfortunately, he did not have the time to pursue his dreams of a professional baseball career. Although he was stymied at the time by his ambition of being a professional baseball player, he never forgot the dream. He spent a year managing a Jack in the Box in California. He then left the state for a year, where he spent time in Denver, Colorado. There, he met his biological father and learned a new skill as a carpenter. He then returned to California, where he was able to join and become part of a semi-pro industrial league team. Michael quickly found he had not lost the skills he had acquired earlier in his life. He was, once again, right back in the thick of it, and his dream to go for the big league was back in play.

Michael could run like a deer, and he had a very strong and accurate throwing arm. Here is another story you might not believe, but again, it is an incredible one indeed.

In a particular game, Michael was playing center field. The game was close when the opposing team's best batter came up to the plate. He was a big strapping fellow, and Michael knew he could blast a long ball if he connected with it. As I said, he was the star hitter for the opposing team. In this game, they were not playing their regular home field. It had been flooded because of a major water leak. Parks and recreation had acquired an alternate field for them to play on. This field had no outfield fence to it.

Michael had positioned himself just back of where the fence would have been in a regular field. It was here he would make a catch that would be the highlight of his baseball career. The batter lined up beside the plate and waved his bat several times as he waited on the pitch. The pitcher made his wind up and hurled a 90 mph fastball at the catcher's mitt. The batter swung hard, and the bat made a loud cracking sound as it connected solidly to that fastball. Michael had moved back a good extra 30 feet from where the fence would have been, just in case the guy slammed it. Well, he had crushed it all right. Michael watched the ball as it arched high out over center field. He quickly realized it was going to take much longer than he had anticipated. He turned and began running in the direction of the ball travel while looking back over his shoulder. The ball was coming down but well over his head. It was on the opposite side of where he was looking. At the last possible moment, Michael launched his body forward, his arm fully outstretched with his open glove skyward. He dived face-first into the ground. The crowd erupted as the ball fell into his open glove. It was a truly magnificent catch, and the batter is out. It was probably the longest out in baseball at well over 450 feet. Michael had an amazing game. He had an amazing catch, threw out a runner from center field at home base, and batted three base hits, two singles, and a triple. Any major leaguer would have been proud of that performance.

After he had made the catch for the final out of the inning, he was sitting in the dugout waiting for his turn at bat. He notices the manager of the other team walking towards him through his team's dugout. He walks up and stops in front of Michael. He puts out his hand to shake Michael's. He then tells Michael he has come to thank the player who had given him the privilege of witnessing the greatest catch he had ever seen in all his years of baseball. It was a beautiful compliment and gratifying moment for Michael. This was also the one game that his father and sister, Christie, came to watch, so it made it that much more special for Michael. It seemed that he was on his way to the professional Leagues. It was not too long after he made one error that cost him the possibility of going down that career path. Michael arrived late to a practice session. He didn't have time to get his normal warm-up session done. Just before starting infield practice, the batter hit a bouncer out toward third base, where Michael was playing. Michael picked it up on the first hop and then made a hard throw to first. As he threw, he suddenly felt a searing, sharp pain in his shoulder. He knew he had done some serious damage. He moved from third base to second so he wouldn't have to throw as hard to first, but his shoulder was still very painful. The pain did not go away after several days, so he made an appointment to go see a sports doctor. The doctor took some X-rays and then presented Michael with the bad news. He had a severely torn rotator cup and shoulder muscle. The doctor told him he probably should get surgery to repair it. Even with the surgery, he would probably not have the full use of his arm. Michael did not want surgery, so he decided to see how it would heal on its own. In a few weeks, he came back to play and gave it a try. He played second base again, so he would not have to throw as hard to first base to get out. It still really hurt. Michael decided to give up playing as he felt he could no longer fully contribute to the team the way things were. His baseball career aspirations had come to an end. He was not a very happy leprechaun with this situation.

Michael, although he could not play anymore, was asked by his Aunt Helen to coach a little league team. When he took over the team, some of the best players had been taken by other teams, and players of lesser ability were put back in. When Michael saw this, he realized he needed to educate his team on the fundamentals before they hit the field. He worked out with a local school the use of a classroom for a few weekends. There, he could use a on the chalkboard. He could demonstrate on the on the chalkboard various pointers for playing the game with the players. They would better understand the rules before they started actual practice. By using his knowledge gleaned from knowing and playing the game since being a little leaguer himself, he was able to bring them to a second-place finish. At the end of the season, they had an end-of-year celebration. They played the winning team and beat them. His knowledge of the game was on the money, and the leprechaun was able to give back so others could learn and enjoy the game.

I mentioned earlier that Michael loved to play golf and, in fact, could have been a scratch golfer. He still has beautiful swing that several others have remarked on and I can attest to it as well. He didn't get to play very much after he was married as he was running his restaurant, a Jack in the Box, full-time to support his wife and kids. He had been working straight for many months without a break. One afternoon in the middle of the week, when it was a little slower and lunch was over, he decided to hit some balls at a nearby golf course and driving range. He was hitting the balls on a beautiful sunny day and enjoying himself. He was one of a few at the range. He noticed there was someone giving golf lessons a ways off but did not pay much attention to it.

Sometime later, he notices a guy standing a little way off, watching him hit the balls. It turns out he was the head pro who worked at the course. He told Michael he had been watching him for a while and remarked that Michael had a beautiful swing. He still does. He wondered if he had ever thought about playing the game professionally.

Michael told him no; he just liked to play when he could but didn't have the time because of his work commitments, as he had a family to look after.

A couple of weeks later, Michael again decided to go hit some more balls at the driving range. He was striking the ball beautifully. He didn't realize he was being watched from the pro shop. The pro came down and asked him if he could watch Michael hit the balls. Michael said sure. He asked Michael if he knew how to slice the ball. He explained to Michael that sometimes you might need to do a slight slice to go around a bend or an obstacle on the course. He then demonstrated to Michael how to strike the ball to get the fade. Michael quickly picked it up, and the pro was very impressed. He then showed Michael how to hook or draw the ball. Again, Michael picked it up quickly and made it look easy. After Michael had finished, the pro told Michael once more he felt he was good enough to go on tour. He would just need to get some sponsors to get him started. Michael told him again that he could not take the risk of giving up his business. He had a family he needed to look after. We will never know for sure whether he would have made a big success of it, but based on his many other successes, he probably would have made a decent go of it. Michael eventually reached a point where he was not able to do a full swing. His other shoulder was seriously damaged when he was kicked by one of his horses.

Although Michael cannot fully swing a golf club, he still has the ability and finesse to pitch very accurately and putt the ball. He has great observational skills. He has the ability to teach others how to improve their game and be better golfers. I can speak personally to that. Here is another interesting story that shows his skill. Two older ladies, sisters, came into his store at the marketplace to buy some sun visors and other golf accessories.

One had been golfing for some time, and the other had limited golf experience. In conversation with them, they told him they were going to be playing in a tournament in the near future at the Talking Stick resort with 100 other women golfers. Michael offered to give them a little coaching if they were interested. They gladly took him up on the offer. Michael made the time to meet them at the Talking Stick course, where he tutored them for a couple of days. He forgot all about it until one day, sometime later, one of the sisters came rushing into his store. She excitedly exclaimed that she and her sister had come in 1st and 2nd in the golf tournament. It was a very nice validation of his coaching skills. First and second! Do you believe it? It has never happened before in the history of golf that we know of.

Michael also loved to play the game of basketball. He was quite short for a basketball player but was very accurate in inputting the ball through the hoop. Being short was not a deterrent to being a very excellent team player. Being a leprechaun to boot didn't hurt at all as well.

Because of his strong arm and his great eye and hand coordination, he could play the hoop and the backboard with equal precision. He and his brother liked to play on the same team as they worked very well together. He, unfortunately, had to stop playing basketball for some time. He had a major injury to his ankle, where he almost lost his foot. He was playing in a game when he jumped up high on a rebound. When he came back down, he twisted, and his foot was out of place. He came down on the foot of an opposing player. Michael's ankle and foot twisted, and his foot dislocated. It twisted almost completely around a hundred and eighty degrees in the opposite direction. It looked freaking ugly. The pain was excruciating. Every bump on the way to the hospital took on a whole new meaning. When they arrived at the hospital, it was immediately being worked on. Unfortunately, the way it had twisted, the circulation had been cut off, and the foot was swelling and turning blue.

The doctor told him that the foot might have to be amputated. Michael was devastated. How could he play sports if he lost a foot? Michael begged him not to take off the foot, to do everything he could to save it. Michael felt his life would be ruined if he lost his foot.

The doctor agreed that they would try to save it but could not promise it. He told Michael that because of what they were going to try, they would have to knock him out as the process would be very painful. Michael would find out later that a crew had worked on it for quite some time. The muscles had locked up, and they had to gently massage back and forth until the muscles loosened to a point where it was able to be twisted back straight.

Michael woke up some hours later and felt pain in the area of his injured ankle and foot. He could not see his feet as they were under the covers. Oh no, he thought, *did I lose my foot?* He was afraid to look. A nurse came in, and Michael asked her to look and see if he still had two feet. She lifted the blanket and told him, yes indeed, he still had two feet. Michael breathed a huge sigh of relief. This experience turned out to be a major turning point in Michael's life. Michael has told me he could play any sport, so long as it didn't involve skis or skates of any kind.

After his foot had healed Michael was back to playing basketball. He was in a league, and it was down to the Championship game. The teams were tied with 16 seconds to go. The opposing team scores and there are three seconds on the clock. His team gets the ball. His teammate sees Michael around center court. He fires a bullet towards him. Michael grabs the ball, takes two steps forward and launches the ball towards his opponents net. The buzzer goes off as the ball leaves his hands. It sails through the air and swishes through dead center of the basket tying the game. The teams go into overtime and Michael's team wins the championship. Nice turn around.

Michael always wondered where the high interest in sports came from. The father who raised him had no interest or apparent ability in that facet of life.

It wasn't until he met his biological father, who, it turned out, was quite the jock. He had been the athlete of the year at his high school. Michael twigged on possibly where much of his desire and genetic ability came from.

Here is another fun story you may find hard to believe. As stated earlier, Michael has an amazing ability of hand and eye coordination. It wasn't long after he had been married, he took his wife Margie out to the Del Mar Fair in San Diego. It happened to be near where they lived. They wandered around the fair, taking in the sights and sounds. Eventually, they found themselves at the fair carnival. There were many games of skill where you could test your abilities. If you were good enough, you could win a prize of your choice. In many cases, it was a large stuffed animal. They soon found themselves in front of a throwing game. It had three metal milk bottles set up on a shelf, about twelve to fifteen feet away. Two bottles were on the bottom, and the third one sat on the top of the bottom two. You bought one baseball for a dollar. If you knocked all three down with your ball, you won a small prize of your choice. You had to hit them in the lower center as one of the bottles was weighted. If you were off slightly, all three would not go down. When you did knock them down, you received a small prize. If you repeated it again with one more ball and knocked all six, you could have your choice of any prize. If you missed the second, you had to give back your first smaller prize.

Michael would buy his ball, throw it, and would knock over the three bottles. He would then repeat with one more and knock over the three more. He and his wife Margie were collecting armfuls of large stuffed animals. He was so good that in short order, he had a big crowd around just watching him repeat his performance. The carnie running the game finally said he couldn't play anymore.

Michael was ready to leave with both his and Margie's arms being stuffed with the plush animals. An older man, a grandfather, and his grandson had been watching for some time. The grandfather asks Michael if he would throw one for him to win his grandson a prize. Michael sizes up the situation and agrees to do so.

The old man buys a ball and hands it to Michael. Before the carnie could object, Michael had thrown it and knocked over three more bottles. Can you do one more, the old man asks, to get my grandson a bigger prize? Michael told him he could throw another one, but if he missed, he would have to give back the smaller prize. His grandson would have nothing. The grandfather tells him, "Go ahead, I am sure you can do it." Michael throws it. Of course, he knocks them down to win the big prize. The leprechaun came through for Grandpa. Now it was really time to go home. As they are leaving the carnival grounds, just near the entrance and exit, there is another throwing game of skill. The carnie running it sees Michael and Margie with their arms full of winning prizes. He starts badgering him and taunting him. Michael ignores him, but the guy keeps on calling after him, saying he could never win there. He just won't give it up. By now, it is quite dark out. They are now a good distance away, but the guy still does not let up. Okay, enough is enough, Michael says to himself. He tells Margie he is going to make the carnie eat crow.

Now this game has six furred characters set up in a straight line about six inches apart on three separate rows. You buy three balls. You must knock down three to get the prize. A big white snoopy dog was the top and only prize.

Michael says to him, "With this one dollar, I am going to knock three down in a row, and I am going to let you pick them out. If I knock one down, you didn't choose, I lose.

When I do knock them down, you are going to give me that snoopy dog right there." Michael emphatically points to it. The carnie is now looking a bit nervous and not so much a smart ass but agrees.

He points out the first one. Michel throws and down it goes. The guy points out the next one. Once again, Michael easily knocks it over. All right, tell me the third one Michael barks at the carnie. The carnie points it out, Michael throws, and down it goes. Michael now barks at him quite loudly, "Now, give me my Snoopy Dog." The subdued carnie, somewhat in shock, gingerly passes it over. Michael and Margie finally leave, with their arms overloaded with a varied collection of stuffed animals. The carnie was probably wondering after Michael left, who was that guy? He is probably still telling the story to all those who come to try to beat the odds. He may be a little more careful about who he eggs on. The lesson here is it is not a good idea to heckle and harass a leprechaun, you just might regret it. This is just another, believe it or not, tale.

Michael never achieved his dream of being a professional athlete but has never lost his interest or love of sports. He keeps himself up to date on the standings of baseball, football, basketball and golf. If not for injuries at a young age, his life would probably have taken a completely different turn. But then, there wouldn't be all these tales to tell. Today, at 80, Michael can't fully swing a golf club, but he can pitch and putt with the best. He has actually came up with simple scientific methods to teach any golfer to improve their short game when it comes to pitching and putting. Michael actually won a major putting contest some years ago at a Golf Fest show he participated in.

He is currently working on creating a series of videos to demonstrate how his methods work. They will probably end up making him another pot of gold. You will probably find them on Amazon.

As the Author and one of his students, I have watched him bring this new project to fruition. Now you know a little more about this possible leprechaun and his athletic abilities.

Michael—The Entrepreneur

The spirit of the entrepreneur is very much alive and well in this leprechaun. As I write his story, he is going on 80 and is still going strong. His current project is running a busy shop at a very large marketplace in Mesa, Arizona. There, he sells many things related to the game of golf. He also has the largest selection of ball caps. His main line is military hats of all the US forces. It has been a more than successful venture. He originally created it for his son Patrick, who did very well with it. But after a couple of years, he decided he would go in a different direction. It has now become Michael's latest successful venture. Michael, in all his endeavours of selling products to retailers or to the end consumer, has to have, what he calls the four "Happys", to be very successful.

First, can the supplier sell it to a distributor at a price both the supplier and the distributor are happy with? Second, could the distributor sell it to the retailer where they both are happy? Third, can the retailer sell it at a price he can be happy with? Fourth, is it at a price where the consumer is happy and believes he or she is getting it at a fair price? There is also an important fifth point that also applies. Is it a product that has wide public appeal?

Michael's entrepreneurship started at a very young age. He and his brother Don took on a paper route. They also were doing landscaping and taking care of their neighbours' yards. They always did a very professional job and developed many happy repeat customers. When he was only 16, his older brother was able to help him get a job working in a local burger joint. This was after he finished a short stint of working in a local movie theatre as an usher.

Michael is a fast learner and soon had the art and skill of being a very successful short-order cook. The owner was so impressed with his abilities he made him the manager. He managed the burger joint very successfully. At the time, he was just seventeen years of age. As with everything he does in his life, Michael is a perfectionist. He works to enhance his skills, so he becomes highly proficient at whatever venture he undertakes.

The night his father kicked them both out, his brother said, "Let's go up to Los Angeles. I know a guy I had earlier trained to manage a Jack in the Box. He now owns his own store. I will get him to hire us on." Michael was game, so away they headed that early morning.

His brother Don landed a job, but Michael did not. Michael told his brother, "Don't worry, I will find another one and get myself hired on."

Michael went out the next day and found another J&B nearby In Burbank. He meets the owner and interviews for a job. The owner tells him the hourly wage he pays his staff. Being a leprechaun and knowing his abilities, Michael tells the owner I am worth more than that, and I will prove it to you. Being the character he is, he makes the owner an offer he couldn't refuse. Michael tells him, "Let me work a shift for nothing, to show just what I am capable of. If I handle things to your satisfaction, give me a job at the pay I ask for. If I don't, you will be out nothing." This catches the owner's attention, so he goes for the offer. He is sure Michael will definitely not be able to deliver on his promises. The next day, Michael shows up to work for the afternoon-evening shift. It was a Friday, the busiest shift of the week. The owner tells him it takes three people to run the grill efficiently. He is told there are two other employees to work with him on the grill. Michel tells him he does not need any help, but he can keep them there if he wants to. He says he can effectively manage it on his own. Of course, the owner is super sceptical and tells him that is not possible. He says he will keep them there on the possibility they are needed. Michael runs the full grill by himself for the complete shift. Everything goes off without a hitch. The owner, who has been watching all evening, tells Michael to please show up at his office at 8 am the next day. When Michael arrives the next morning, he heads upstairs to the owner's office to meet with him and to get his badge. They exchange pleasantries with each other. The owner then says to him, "Last night, I have never seen the likes of what you did with that complete evening shift. I am still having difficulty believing what I, in fact, witnessed."

Not only is Michael hired, but sitting on the desk is a company badge with Michael's name on it. It also says assistant manager. Michel also receives the pay he has wanted. Now, just so you know, this is completely out of the norm for becoming the assistant manager. It just doesn't happen that way. It normally takes months, at the very least, to become an assistant manager. Most, when already in that position, stay in for a long time. Only a possible leprechaun could just walk into that position after just doing one shift.

Michel is so good at his job he is soon training all the new staff. The manager would leave Michael to run the restaurant on his own while he left for the afternoon to bank and go play golf. Michael worked at the store for over a year. His brother, in the meantime, had been drafted into the army. Michael no longer had his brother, his best friend, nearby him. He really didn't have anyone else he really knew or was close to in the area. He decides to take a break from it all. He makes a call to his aunt on his adopted father's side. She and her husband, the police chief, were living up in Denver. Michael asks her if it would be okay to come and visit for a couple of weeks so he can clear his head. Maybe he could decide what he might want to do with his life going forward. His aunt tells him, yes, of course, she would love to have Michael come and visit. One early morning, after he had been there for a week or two, his aunt asked him if he had ever wanted to meet his biological father. Michael tells her, no, not really, he doesn't even know where he lives. His aunt tells him that his father lives a few houses away, down on the corner. She tells him, "You drive by it on the way here every day."

Michael becomes curious when He drives by the house. His curiosity finally gets the better of him. He gets up his nerve to go pay him a visit.

A few days later, he walks up and knocks at the door. His father's wife answers. He introduces himself, and he hears his father yell from within the house, "Who is it?" She yells back, "It is a fellow named Michael, says he is your son." His father comes to the door and tells him to come in. During his visit, he finds out he has two younger step sisters who have been told they have two half-brothers living somewhere in CA. The oldest one, who is about 16, has been enamoured with the idea of having an older brother. She quickly becomes his biggest fan. After some chit-chat conversation has taken place, his father asks Michael what his plans are. Michael, at this point, says he does not have anything definite. His father, who is a general building contractor in Denver, tells him if he is possibly interested, they could go down to the local carpenters union office. There, he could sign up as a carpenter apprentice. He would have an opportunity to learn a new and useful trade. His father, being a successful contractor, had all the right connections and knew all the ins and outs of the general construction industry.

Michael thinks about it a little and decides why not. He takes him up on the offer. The next day, his father takes him down to the local Carpenters Union Office, where he is soon officially signed up as a carpenter apprentice.

Hie and his father then went to a local hardware store and bought him the basic tools and needs to get started. He also gave him his original wooden toolbox he started with. Michael thought that was really thoughtful of him. In short order, he has his first job. His father offers him a place to stay until he is settled. He is welcome to have a room in the upscale basement apartment. Michael gratefully accepts and moves in. He has decided to find his own job rather than work for his father. It makes him feel more of his own person, independent and less beholden to anyone. Michael doesn't stay at his father's house for very long. As mentioned earlier, he lived down in the basement. One late evening, an incident occurred in the house that had nothing to do with him directly. It makes him decide that it would be best for everyone's sake if he moves out. The next day, he finds a room to rent that is close by. It is in a quiet neighbourhood run by a retired couple, where he happily stays until he heads back to California.

There is another interesting thing that occurred concerning his relationship with his newfound father. When he first came to Denver, he had a 56 Chevy convertible, which he really liked. His father said he would help him get a newer car. Michael liked his old car, but his father insisted, so he traded in his car and left the dealership with a newer one. This would be the object of upset and contention in the not too far future. He had no driveway to park his car at his new place, so he parked on the street. The winter was quite cold, and there was plenty of snow. He woke up one morning and looked out to where the car was parked. He couldn't even see it. It was covered with snow higher than its roof. Before he could go to work, it would take some time just to be able to get the car freed up. The snow on the street was very wet and slushy from all the cars going by.

Michael tells himself to be very careful not to fall. He ends up falling on his butt three times as he works to clear the snow from off and around his car. To add insult to injury, the street was one-way and was becoming busier and busier with the morning commuting traffic.

He was very soon soaked to the skin by wet slush as each car went by and splashed the slush on him. He finally had his car free. He goes back into his room to get out of his wet, cold clothes. When he finally starts to warm up, he thinks of what he has just gone through. He makes an executive decision. He is not going to go back out into that miserable winter weather with the possibility of slipping and falling 18 stories off the building he was working on. Michael heads back to bed and stays there for a good part of the day. He had pleasant dreams of warm sunny days in southern California. He was no Eskimo, he was a warmth-seeking leprechaun.

One morning, some weeks later, he was getting ready to go to work. He looks out and sees his car is not parked on the street. He thinks it must have been stolen. He calls up his aunt, whose husband, Uncle Harold, happens to be the police chief of Denver. When he tells his aunt his car has been stolen, she says, "No, Michael, it's in your father's driveway." It turned out his father had come and taken the car back in the middle of the night. After that occurred, he didn't speak with his father for many years.

We will go over what happened with his relationship with his biological father in a later chapter. His aunt had called her brother, his father, in California and told him what had happened with Michael. His father, who had kicked him and his brother out earlier, calls him up and tells him to go pick out any car he wants. He will co-sign for him. Michael ends up getting a new 65 Mustang.

His first job in Denver was working on a complex called Windsor Apartments. He is quickly beginning to learn the ins and outs of the carpenter trade. One morning, Michael is working by himself, cutting 2x4s for a particular job. The superintendent had been around inspecting and had left, or so Michael thought. While he was working, Michael felt that someone was watching him. He turned and looked behind to see if, in fact, that was the case. He spots the construction super standing behind some uprights a couple of rooms away. He was peering through the open wall and putting his attention on Michael. This really annoys him. If the guy wants to observe him, let him come over and watch, not doing it kind of covertly from afar. Michael saws off a 3 to 4-inch piece of the 2x4, whirls around, and, in a continuous smooth motion, fires it off, with his accurate baseball arm, in the direction of the super. It goes whizzing by him, just missing, and clatters around the room. One second, he is there, and the next, he is not. Michael figures he will be fired but never hears a word about it. Just so you know, leprechauns do not like to be spied upon.

His second job is at a Safeway store. Here, he meets two journeyman carpenters, Dwayne and Richard, who take him under their wings and help him be successful in his new chosen field. It was on this job that he fell through the roof, which almost cut short his carpentry career and his life as well. He and another carpenter were working up about thirty feet, strengthening the support struts for a new roof on the Safeway store. They had set up two 4 x 8 sheets of plywood butted back-to-back across the roof support rafters. The roof was otherwise completely open. Michael and his coworker are working facing in opposite directions off the two sheets of plywood. They keep on moving them down the length of the roof together.

As they are getting near the end of the roof, his partner moves his sheet without letting Michael know. When Michael backs up, he steps off his sheet into the open air. He now finds himself falling straight down through the building interior towards the floor, some thirty feet below. Michael said his whole life flashed before him. In mere seconds. He surely thought his number was up. He came to a very sudden and abrupt, jarring stop as he ended up straddling a large cowling covering a cooling motor in the refrigeration section of the store.

Being a leprechaun, he survives, but he finds it almost impossible to sit down for several weeks. He couldn't go to work for a couple of months. It is interesting to note how he obtained this next job. As was related earlier, on this second job, he had met these two brothers, Dwayne and Richard, who happened to be very experienced carpenters and contractors. They took a liking to young Michael. After the fall through the Safeway roof, Michael had been off work for some time. That job he had been on had now been completed. Late one afternoon, Michael was driving in the downtown area of Denver. He spots a car ahead of him that appears to be like the one belonging to his friend Richard. He pulls up beside him at a stop light and sees it is Indeed Richard. He taps his horn to get his attention. They both roll down their windows and exchange greetings.

Richard asks Michael how he is doing and if he is now ready to go back to work. Michael tells him yes; he is ready to go. Richard tells him to report to the field office at the thoroughbred racetrack in Littleton first thing in the morning. Michael thanks him and tells him he will be there. At 8 am the next morning, he shows up at the construction office where Richard is waiting with the field super. Richard tells the super he is hiring Michael and is to start him 25 cents an hour over base wage. Wow, Michael is more than pleased with his new situation.

Two weeks later, Michael gets his first pay check. The superintendent hands Michael his check. As Michael takes his check, the super says to him, "Where is my bottle?" Michael is confused and asks him what he is talking about. The super then tells Michael to follow him over to his station wagon. When they get close to it, Michael sees it is loaded with bottles. He says you need to add a bottle. Michael retorts, "I know where you can get a bottle, the liquor store, so go get your own bottle. I am not buying you a bottle." The next thing Michael hears is, you are fired. Michael walks over to see Richard. Richard asks him how it is going. Michael tells him he has just been fired. Richard is taken aback and asks what happened. Michael relates to him what has just transpired. Richard is very upset and can't believe it. He tells Michael, "Come with me."

They walk into the super's office, and Richard barks at him. "Did you tell this guy he had to buy you a bottle, and when He said no, you fired him?" The guy mumbles yes. Richard very emphatically says to him, "You are hiring this guy back with a 50c an hour raise. If you don't, 167 Carpenters will not be working on this site tomorrow." It felt very good to have someone with authority on his side. Richard was the union steward over all the carpenters working there.

Within a week, the super was gone, and Richard was now the acting superintendent. Was this the luck of a leprechaun!? This was the job where he fell off a scaffold fifteen feet above the ground. His luck held out, and he was not injured. The plank on the scaffold he was working off was only Very slightly overlapping with the enjoining plank. It was barely tacked in with nails, so it was not properly secured. With bouncing occurring from walking back and forth on the plank, the nails pulled free. The plank now came off the one end of the scaffold and over he went. He was bruised but not seriously injured. The carpenters who were responsible for this were fired. Michael continued to work, becoming more and more efficient in the trade. He was becoming a very able carpenter apprentice. Richard, the new superintendent, tells Michael to come and see him first thing each morning. He asks him to tell him where he is going to be working and then go and work on any part of the job he wishes. Just let me know where you are going to be, so I know. That way, Michael would quickly learn much more than if he just kept working on the same thing over and over. As a note, when you are a carpenter, you are independent. You can choose to work where and when you want, especially if you are good and capable at what you do. While he was in Denver, his younger stepsister and he became quite close. I spoke with her as part of doing this story. I asked her how she felt about her new older brother. She spoke very enthusiastically about him. She told me how he had taught her to swing a hot bat and become a proficient hitter playing softball. He also coached her on how to handle a pool cue with finesse. I heard from her very enthusiastic response that she obviously thought VERY highly of him. They are still very close to this very day and communicate with each other on a regular basis.

Michel stayed there and worked through his first Denver winter. The weather had been beautiful at 75 F until one late October day. He had gone to work in shorts and a tee shirt.

Michael had never experienced any real cold weather growing up in southern California. He was eagerly anticipating his first snow. Well, it soon turned into a very cold day. The temperature dropped 45 degrees in an hour, and it kept dropping. Then, the snow came, and the wind along with it. It turned out to be a record-breaking drop in temperature in a one-hour period. It certainly was not the romantic image he had envisioned. He was wearing just a tee shirt and shorts. He froze his butt off that day, working 18 stories up. He made a firm decision that day. If he made it through the winter, it would be the last winter he worked in Denver. He would be going back to California when the first snowfall arrived the next season. He worked and suffered through the cold Denver winter. He worked through the spring, summer, and into the next fall season until November rolled around once more. It was a Friday, the end of the week and payday. The snow started to flutter down, and Michael knew it was time for him to go. At lunch, he informs his boss that he is leaving, this will be his last day. His boss thinks he is just kidding and asks why he wants to be leaving now.

Michael points to the snowflakes feathering down and says, there's the reason as he points to the falling snow. At the end of the day, when his boss hands him his pay check, he says to Michael, "We'll see you Monday, right?" Michael tells him no and thanks him for being able to work for him, but he is going to be heading southwest back to sunny California. Michael, true to his word, hits the road back to southern California that very day.

The next day, Michael arrives back in the San Diego area but with no place to call home. He drives down to a local mobile home park and goes into the manager's office. He asks if he has a cheap trailer to rent. The manager said yes, there is an 18-footer just down at the end of the park, and it rents cheaply. Michael drives over and does a quick inspection. It certainly isn't fancy, but it will be satisfactory for his needs for the time being. It is mainly a place to lay his head at night, and the price is right. He tells the park manager he'll take it. He pays for a month's rent and heads for the door. The manager says to him as he is about to leave, "Someone will be down shortly to turn on the gas." Michael replies, "Don't worry about it. I will get it working." He drives down to the trailer and parks out front, about 10 to 12 feet from the entrance to the trailer. The door opens directly in the middle of the trailer, facing towards the side of his parked car. He can see that there is a gas stove against the wall facing the door. Michael walks behind the trailer, where the tank is located. He turns on the gas, then comes back around to the front. He goes in to light the pilot light on the stove. He finds the valve to turn on the gas and opens it up. He gets out a match and puts it down by the pilot light. It doesn't light, and the match goes out. He repeats this several times without getting it going. He then gets up and goes back out to check the tank to make sure there is fuel and that the valve is open. It all seems to be in order. He returns back around and enters the trailer to give it one more try. He walks into the trailer and strikes a match as he begins to bend down towards the stove. Immediately, there is a loud, deafening, bright orange flash and a deafening explosion. Michael is blasted through the open door and completely out of the trailer. He flies through the air and lands on top of his car 10 to 12 feet away. His eyebrows and much of his hair are burned off, and he can't see. His ears are ringing like a bell. He is completely stunned and confused, to say the least.

Surprisingly, nothing is broken, and he does not sustain any major damage, only minor burns. In a few days, his eyesight returns to normal, and his ears stop ringing. It takes a little longer for his eyebrows and hair to grow back. This is another unbelievable story of escaping death's door. Are you starting to wonder? Shaken but no serious injury. The trailer did not burn up, and there was actually not much damage done. If things had been configured differently, this story would probably never have been told. Looking back on it, Michael feels the Angels were watching over him. Maybe leprechauns have more than their share. Needless to say, he found another place to stay. This time, it was with no gas. Michael swore he would never have gas in any house he lived in from that time forward. He has kept that promise to himself. Michael was soon back to work, continuing with his carpentry trade now that he was living back in warm, sunny California. He continued to be very busy with this for the next four years.

He continued to demonstrate his skill and proficiency. During this period, he won the prestigious "Carpenter Apprentice of the Year" award for Southern California. Originating from that, here is another story that shows the luck of a leprechaun. Michael had just finished a job after he returned from his winning Carpenter Championship. One early morning, he was driving near the downtown San Diego area when he saw a truck parked outside a new building that was going up. He recognizes the truck. It belongs to the guy who came in second in the carpenter competition. He pulls in, parks his vehicle, and then goes into the building. The carpenter working there recognizes Michael. He is surprised and happy to see him. He asks Michael how he is doing and what he is working on. Michael tells him he just finished a job and is on the lookout for new work. His fellow carpenter says, "Would you like to work on this one? I could use some help here."

Michael fetches his tools from his vehicle and is back to work. A couple of hours later, while he is working his new job, a truck pulls in behind his vehicle. It turns out it is the general contractor in charge of the building he is now working on. Michael introduces himself, and the contractor recognizes him as the person who has just won the recent Carpenters Award. He tells Michael to come over to his truck. He has something he wants Michael to see. He reaches in through the window and grabs a thick, rolled-up set of plans. He tells Michael to take them home, look them over, and then meet him at the address on the plans first thing tomorrow morning. Michael thinks to himself, this seems like a lot of plans just to build a house. That evening, he opens the plans and sees why they are so thick. It certainly is not an ordinary structure that is to be built. It is a two-story with many more complicated things to be done than just a normal single story. After he has studied them thoroughly, he figures he can get it done. This was to be the home of the top architect in southern California. At 8 am the next morning, he meets with the contractor at the site.

He asks Michael what he thinks. Michael tells him he can get it done. He is told, good, it is now his job to complete. Michael oversees the contract and will be ordering all the materials needed to get the job done. He will be in charge of the subcontractors working on the job. Wow, Michael thinks to himself. When the contractor leaves, Michael takes the plans and walks around the exterior of the masonry substructure on which the building is to be erected. He compares the distances of placements of doors, windows, and other features from the drawings he has in his hands. Out front, there are masonry workers building three concrete pillars that will go all the way to the second-floor roof overhang. He looks at the plans and immediately notices that the physical pillars are, in fact, being built two feet off center to where the plans show they should be built. He walks over to the lead mason.

He points out the fact that they are out of place according to the plans. The fellow quickly looks, half acknowledges the fact, but then goes back with his workers and just continues. They already have the pillars up to over six feet. They are not just out of place, but the work is very shoddy looking as well. He has to stop this now. He needed to get in touch with the subcontractor in charge of the masonry work. Just as he is about to call him, the guy drives up. Michael shows him the error according to the plans. The contractor sees that, in fact, all three pillars are misplaced by two feet from where the plans show they should be. Michael tells him that all three will have to be taken out and redone in their correct positions. Since they are built on a large concrete base, they will have to get a crane in to lift them out. It is a very costly mistake indeed. Michael was put in charge of the whole project just after finishing his apprenticeship. He is a quick learner and, thanks to his earlier mentors, has learned many things that would usually not be part of a normal apprenticeship over such a short time. The crane comes in and lifts out the pillars and their bases from the ground. The work has to be redone with the pillars in their proper place.

In the meantime, Michael has ordered all the materials to frame up the house and is getting to work. The general contractor who hired him has hired a couple of labourers to help him. They just happen to be a couple of star players from the hometown hockey team, the San Diego Gulls, the team of whom Michael is a big fan. That was the team they went to watch on their wedding night. Back then, hockey players didn't get top dollar, so they had to work outside their careers to supplement their income.

A few days later, after the forms were set up, he again inspected to see how the new pillars were coming. He is shocked to see the slipshod way they are being made again. The finish is very rough and uneven, not smooth where it can just be painted over. They are up about six feet, and Michael tells them to stop. He was going to call their boss again. Just as he is about to call, he drives up. Their boss seems to be taken aback by their unprofessional-looking work. Michael tells him the pillars will have to be redone again. Out comes the crane and lifts them out. The three masons are sent off and replaced with three new guys. This time, they are finally done right. Somebody on that Job certainly didn't make much money.

That contractor certainly wasn't a leprechaun. Michael finished the job in about three months. He was very pleased with his work, as were the general contractor and the new owner of the house. It had been quite an undertaking for the young carpenter, but the leprechaun had done his magic again. He had done it so well that there was almost no waste after the job was completed.

After completing that job, Michael had basically done the work of a contractor. He told his wife he was thinking about getting his contractor's license. He went down to the local licensing office to find out what he needed to do to obtain a license. While he was there, he saw some of the other carpenters he knew. They were also there to see how to get contractor's licenses. These were also some of the previous apprentices he had competed against. Michael felt what he had observed of their experience and quality were not up to the standard he held. If he had to compete against them, he would be competing against others who would likely be underbid and would not be able to get the job done. So, for the time being, he decided to hold off on getting licensed as a contractor.

At about the same time, his brother, who now had his own Jack in the Box, let Michael know that there was a good possibility of being able to get him one also to lease to own. Don was back from the military and, through his earlier connections, had obtained his own Jack in the Box to lease to own. He had originally trained the owner of a J&B, who now was the CEO of the company. Don talked to the CEO, whom he knew well, and asked him if he could get a store for his brother, too. The CEO gave the okay, and Michael was now into a new venture with his own restaurant. This is not the normal way things are done. Again, his brother Don came through for this leprechaun.

The next part is the unbelievable part, but again, we are talking about a possible leprechaun here. There is a standard training program that all new owners must go through with the corporate office. It normally takes an average of three months or more to be fully trained to run a J&B. The leprechaun pulls it off in 28 days flat. Michael knew a good deal about it from his previous experience as an assistant manager. It is still a record that had never been broken before or happened since. It probably never will be broken and is a testament to his ability and determination.

On finishing the training, he is given his own store in Culver City. This was a very different and eye-opening experience of itself. The last store owner had given it up after just two years. The area where the store was located had gang members partying and dealing drugs in the store parking lot every weekend night. No one would or could be serviced in the evenings because of the gang activity. They would completely take over the place. Again, this is the first J&B that Michael owned and ran. The store had been vandalized many times. The gangs had threatened and intimidated the owner to the point where he said that's it and gave it up. It was just too much severe stress for him. He was not willing to put up with it any longer. The previous owner told Michael some of the things that had happened to him while he was running the restaurant. He told Michael they had threatened his life several times. They shot up Jack's head on top of a high post. They blew up the speaker box on the drive-through and cut the warning line on the drive-through. They would take away the garbage dumpster and move it way down the alley. They would pee on the wall on the walk-up window. They stripped the tree on the property of its leaves. They would leave a ton of garbage to be picked up after they had left for the night. None of it was from J&B.

The first weekend he has the store, Michael tries to prepare for what is to come. It is far worse than he had thought it might be. Just as it begins to get dark out on the Friday evening, the lot starts to fill up. The drinking and the loud partying soon begin. By nine o'clock, every part of the lot, including the drive-through, are all jammed up with cars.

There was no way any paying customers could get in to be serviced. At his back window, there were a couple of parking spots for the owner and the assistant manager. He looked out there and there were cars there as well with open whisky bottles on the hoods. Now remember, we are talking about teenagers here. It was ridiculous. There was drinking, the taking of drugs, loud music, and even a couple of fights going on. Michael immediately calls the Police. Two policemen show up shortly and Michael is hopeful. The gang members were very disrespectful towards the two officers. There are easily a couple hundred people on the lot now. Michael goes out with one officer, and the other goes off to handle some of the crowd.

The one officer is standing beside me talking to a kid. The kid spits a huge loggie in the policeman's face. Michael looks at the cop and sees his hands are shaking. The cops call for back, and soon, more police cars are showing up. A couple of the participants were arrested. The Police finally get the rest of the gang to leave the lot. By ten o'clock, Michael shuts off the lights and tells his staff they are closing as he doesn't feel it is safe for them. After he has closed, his staff has gone home, and the gangs have been cleared out, he goes out to survey his lot. It was like a small hurricane had gone through the place. He starts to pick up the garbage and the many broken and empty bottles. A car comes screeching up. A couple of gang members are yelling expletives at Michael. They yell, "We're going to come and get you for calling the Police. Some of our friends were arrested. They then tear off in a screech of tires and a cloud of burning rubber. They yell at Michael they will be back. It had certainly been an eye-opener for the first week of taking over his new store. He knew he could not continue with this current situation. He would have to do something quickly to ensure it was gotten under control and didn't happen again.

The next morning, early, he went down to the local police station. He demanded to see the Chief. After being made to wait for some time, the Chief finally came out of his office to see him. Michael introduced himself to the Chief as the new owner of the local J &B. He quickly told the Chief he needed police presence to show up to patrol around his restaurant a couple of times in the evenings and, especially on the weekends, when the gang members would regularly come to fill up the parking lot and party.

The Chief told him the previous owner had said no police as he feared for his life. He had been told by the gang on several occasions what would happen if the Police were called. Michael told the Chief, "I am not that owner, and I want the police presence now." That very night, patrol cars started showing up on a regular basis.

This immediately had a positive effect. It wasn't very long before the gang found some other place to hang out to do their partying. That did not stop some of the members of the gang from threatening Michael's life and retaliating by vandalizing various parts of the property over the next year. Despite the rocky beginning, Michael handled a bad situation and turned it into a success.

As a side note, one morning, as he was preparing to open, an older lady knocked on the front ordering window of the store. She said she came to thank Michael for what he did to get rid of the gang from the area. She told him she lived just behind the store parking lot and she had feared for her life on the weekend nights. Her husband worked nights, and she was home alone. She told him she now felt unsafe to go out. Since the gang was gone, she no longer felt afraid.

To that degree, Michael had helped to restore some order and calm in the neighbourhood. What a Good leprechaun. About a year later, he was asked if he wanted to take on a brand-new Palos Verdes store in a real upscale area. He, of course, jumped at it, so he went from the worst area to the best. It was during the time he was running the new store that Jack in the Box Corp was bought out by another large corporation, Ralston Purina. It wasn't very long before all the store owners were called in for an update to meet the new Corp owners. They were all assured nothing would change, that operations would carry on as usual. That, unfortunately, turned out to be a lie. In very short order, major changes came down the pipe, and they were not in the favour of the restaurant owners.

Profits went down, and opportunities for expansion were severely curtailed. This was all done on purpose to make the independent owner stores into all company stores. Michael and many of the other owners had enough of this. Michael and many other owners departed to look for new and brighter opportunities.

It was after this that Michel decided to try a new MLM vitamin business. He poured all his savings into it. He bought a large number of products. As part of it, he went through a training course called Leadership Dynamic Institute. The company was headquartered in Los Angeles while the course was being held in San Francisco. Michael thought it would be about some kind of corporate leadership and something to do and learning to be a better business leader. It turned out to be a very different sort of experience indeed. He told me it turned into war games for a week. He told me it was one of the hardest things he had ever done in his life. Before the course started, they had to be sworn to secrecy to not divulge what the course actually entailed. He left to do the course in business attire.

He returned home with them more or less in tatters. It didn't make him any pot of gold at the time, but the end result of doing that course was that he felt he had the completed equivalent of a master's degree in just one week. The vitamin business itself was just a little ahead of its time. He did come out of that course knowing he could accomplish anything that he set his mind to do. He proved this over and over to himself throughout the rest of his life. It made him into a stronger, better leprechaun than ever before. You will read about more as we go through this book. Each member of the group that completed the course received a silver Genie teapot as a real reminder of what they had  gone through. Here is a picture of it. I guess this is a symbol to remind each one to never put the genie back in the lamp once you release it.

It was after this his cash flow was temporarily non-existent. Michael and his family were cash-poor. For a couple of weeks, they lived on bread and potatoes and had to water down the baby food. It was about that time he made his trip to Holly Wood Park horse racetrack and came home with his pockets stuffed with lots of cash. There is much more detail on that when we talk about Michael In the chapter "The Horse Whisperer." Michael was again looking for a path to create income to support his family. Once again, his brother Don comes to the rescue. Don was now managing a restaurant in a chain called Pioneer Take Out. It was a newer chain. They were quite a successful chicken take out and eat in, in Marina Del Rey seaside.

It is a part of the greater Los Angeles area. The restaurants had a popular menu with good traffic locations. His brother Don, who was now the manager for another owner, Introduced Michael to the president of the new and upcoming franchise. His brother seemed keen on it, so Michael made a down payment and bought into one. Michael, of course, quickly learned the ins and outs of the new restaurant. He soon had it running very successfully, producing good income for many months. One day, his brother Don and the other owner came to see him. This fellow had never been in the restaurant business. He was an Investor who was a head test pilot at Point Mugu Naval Base in southern California. This owner makes a proposal to Michael and his brother. This fellow now had two stores. He invited Michael to put his store into a corporation where he would be part of the larger organization. He would then be part of the expansion as they acquired new stores. He told Michael this would increase their overall buying power. It would make all the newer franchises more valuable. They would all make more money. Michael's brother was to be the coordinator with a new car. Michael was to be the head supervisor. He would then be part of a bigger and growing business, so he signed on to it. A couple of months went by, and there was to be a meeting at their new flagship restaurant up in Camarillo, California.

The fellow had brought a pilot friend who was also going to invest in the business. He didn't ask or even tell Michael or Don this would be happening. While they were sitting at the booth in the restaurant, his brother had to leave to go to the washroom. The other owner tells Michael there are going to be some changes made to the deal. They won't need the car for his brother anymore. He outlines several other major changes he plans to make. Michael nods his head but doesn't say anything.

He thinks to himself, this all sounds like a con job going on. He says nothing to his brother when he returns to the meeting. They agreed to meet at Michael's restaurant about a month later to go over and set up the final agreements. When they have left, he tells his brother what the fellow had told him about making all these changes without any input on their behalf. He tells his brother they need to contact a lawyer to see what they need to do to get out of this situation. Michael and his brother meet with a lawyer a few days later. Michael explains the situation to him. The lawyer tells him he should get out now. He goes over the best way to do it. Michael now goes into action to extricate himself from this questionable deal that he has become involved in. During the next month, before the meeting is to take place, he lets the cash build up. He keeps it in the safe at the restaurant and does not bank it. The day before the meeting, he tells each staff member individually, by telephone, to not come in the next day as they will not be needed. The sly leprechaun was ready for the payback.

The morning of the meeting comes, and Michael takes out the cash from the safe to recoup his initial investment. They lock the keys to the store in the office safe. There were two safes, one inside of the other built into the floor. They put the keys to the car in the dumpster. When the two investors show up just before opening, Michael and his brother meet them inside the store just as they are leaving. Before they leave, Michael tells them that he is giving back the restaurant. He tells them it is because of what was said and done at the meeting in Camarillo. Michael tells them the restaurant is now theirs, to do what they want with it. They chuckle to themselves as they are leaving, envisioning the predicament the investors have now found themselves in. Neither one of them knows anything about operating a restaurant. The store is opening, no staff are coming in, and the keys are all locked away in the safe. You really are taking chances when trying to bamboozle a leprechaun.

The next opportunity once again came through his brother. Don had landed a job managing a restaurant called Pizza Burger. The owner had two stores and was looking to find a new manager to run his other store. Don, of course, told him he should check out his brother. Michael. He meets with the owner and finds that the restaurant is in Fountain Valley. He would have to move out of San Diego. The owner would pay for the move. He would pay Michael a basic salary on what they agreed upon plus a bonus on everything Michael produced over a base set amount. It is funny sometimes how things go full circle. The manager he was replacing was the same person whose Jack in the Box he had taken over in Culver City.

Michael would be in training with his brother at the other location, learning the ins and outs of managing his new store. When he came to start his first day at his own restaurant, the owner started to go over all the necessary steps to setting it up daily and managing the new restaurant on a regular basis.

Michael tells him, to save time, let me do what I think is correct, and you watch and tell me if I leave out or do anything incorrectly. That will show you what I know and what I am missing. This will speed up the process. The owner agreed, and of course, Michael set it up quickly and in the correct order. The owner was very surprised. He asked Michael how he knew what to do. Michael then tells him, "What do you think I have been doing for the last couple of weeks with my brother so I would take over this restaurant."

Michael quickly has his restaurant running efficiently and producing great income. He was quickly hitting home runs. Michael was getting good bonuses on a regular basis. In a few short months, even though the income is still way up, the owner begins cutting back on the bonuses. He keeps reneging on his initial agreements. Michael finally has had enough and quits. His brother follows suit. The two are temporarily out of the restaurant business again. It is interesting to note that not long after the two brothers have left, both restaurants are soon out. Once again, don't fool with a leprechaun when he is making you a pot of gold, you'll probably pay the price, and it won't be in your favour.

As you can see, Michael and his brother were very close. There was a time, however, when he gave his brother an ultimatum in a take-it-or-leave-it situation.

Michael was living in the San Diego area with his wife and their young son. The second one is on the way. Don calls him up to tell Michael his biological father, the one from Denver, whom he has never met, is coming his way. He wants to meet and visit with him. Don is now living in LA County. He asks Michael if he will come up and be there when his father arrives. Michael, based on his earlier experiences, immediately tells him no. He hasn't spoken with his father since

Denver, when his father took back his car. Don keeps pleading with him until Michael finally agrees. It is only because he loves his brother. Don has always been there for him.

The day his father is arriving, he and Margie drive up to his brother's place. They are all sitting in the lobby of the complex where his brother lives. They are watching the walkway for the father to walk up. They see this fellow walking towards the door. "Is that him," Don asks. Michael looks. But at first, he doesn't recognize him. The last time he saw his father, he had completely white hair, but now it is brown. His father had white hair from his late twenties. The father comes in and says hello to them. Then, for the rest of the time, Michael and Margie are left out of the conversation. After a couple of hours, his father tells Michael he would love to meet his grandson. Now Michael's son is back in San Diego at grandma and grandpa's place. It is more than a couple of hours drive each way. Michael is very reluctant to do so, but his father persists. Michael talks it over with Margie. Finally, with some misgivings, he agrees to do so. He drives to San Diego, gets his son, and returns after several hours of driving.

His father pays little or no attention to his grandson once he is there. Michael figures it was just a ruse to get him away so he could talk to Don in private. At the end of the day, Michael and his family leave for home, glad it is over. At least he had been there to support his brother. Before he left, his father apparently asked Don to come out and visit him in Denver, where they could go camping and go fishing in the mountains. Don calls Michael a few days later and asks him if he would come along. Michael again says no. His brother keeps nagging at him until he again agrees, much so against his better judgment.

The day arrives, and they fly out to Denver, where their father picks them up at the airport. Don gets in the front, and Michael is in the back. Michael is completely ignored throughout the drive back to his father's home. It was as if he wasn't there. His brother, unfortunately, seemed to be going along with his father.

The next day, they head to the mountains to go camping and fishing. He is once again ignored on the drive up to the cottage. While they are fishing, his father and Don keep distancing themselves from him. Michael is wise to what is going on with the two of them. Michael does very well with the fishing. His brother and father only catch a couple between them. When they go back to the camp, his father decides he wants to get a picture of Don with the fish. He tells Michael to give his fish to his brother so he can have his picture taken with them. Michael is not a happy camper and says no, take his picture with the fish he caught himself. His father is not happy about his response and tells him, "I don't like your attitude." When they get to the cabin where they will be staying, his father tells Michael to go and get some wood for the fire. By now, Michael is really PO. Michael is really fed up with his father's and his brothers, actions. Michael thinks to himself, I am not your gopher but do go and get the wood. That night, as they are in bed, his father originates a game called the States Game to play before they go to sleep. He will name a state and see who can answer correctly: the capital city.

Michael had studied this in school. He had played this game many times. Michael knew them all by heart. His brother didn't, so Michael came up with all the right answers. His father picked up a bad choice of games to play and accused Michael of being a smart-ass. His father finally told him I am going to drop you off at the bus stop in the morning, and you can take a bus to the airport and go home. This further infuriates Michael. He states to his father, "No, you can drive me to the airport. You brought me here, and you can take me back to the airport yourself." In the morning, they go back to his father's place to pick up his gear. All the way down the mountain, he harasses and harangues his father for his bad attitude. Aside, he tells his brother, when I get on that plane, and if you are not on it with me, then I am through with you as a brother. All the way to the airport, he once again gives his father the, what for, on his attitude and his actions, in dealing with him. When he gets to the airport, his brother boards the plane with him. His brother apologizes several times on the flight home. He never did that to Michael again. He never saw or talked to his biological father again. He and his brother remained very close and on good terms for the rest of their lives.

His brother had caught on; you don't cross a leprechaun. As far as Michael knows, that was the last time his brother ever talked to his biological father.

It was during this period that Michael really started looking at the Spiritual side of his life. We will look at this much more closely in another chapter. It was a major change in Michael's view of life, and he lives it to this very day. After the restaurant period of his life, Michael went back to the trade of being a carpenter.

Because Michael was such a skilled carpenter, he was well-known in the building industry in Southern Cal. When he needed to make money, he could always find part or full-time work to add to his cash flow needs. He would utilize this skill throughout his life, even when he was in the horse business.

In 1978, with the help of his pastor, he opened a very successful leather store called Leather Express. It was in a major shopping center with over 150 stores. Initially, they had been selling mainly leather jackets, but as the business expanded, the store carried many types of high-end leather goods, including purses and a very popular line of women's leather shoes. He and his wife ran this store very successfully through 1982. At that time, a new manager of the mall wanted to take back the section where Michael and several other stores had their stores. He wanted to turn the area into a large food court. To force out the existing vendors, he increased the rent by four times. The store owners there could not afford such an increase in expense, so they all moved out. It was a Friday while he was still working in his leather store. His brother Don came down from LA and asked if he wanted to go play a round of golf. Michael said no, he couldn't that day as he had many orders coming in by UPS.

They could go play the next day on Saturday. Michael showed his brother around the store and pointed out to him a snazzy, upscale line of women's shoes. Don thought they were great. He asks Michael if he could take some of the women's shoes to see if he could sell some. Michael was surprised because his brother was not a salesperson. He was a restauranteur. But Michael was elated to get his brother out of the store so he could get some work done. Michael told him sure, and he could sell them for $10 less than the store as there is no overhead involved. They loaded up his brother's car with many pairs, and off he went. He arrives back later in the afternoon. Michael asks him, how did it go?" Don says, "Good, I sold 18 pairs."

The leprechaun was in a state of disbelief. His brother was a restaurant guy, not a salesman. You sold 18 pairs in a few hours. How did you do that? Where did you go?" I went to hairdressing places, beauty salons, real estate offices, etc. The women loved them, especially when I was selling them for ten dollars less than the stores. Michael was still having a hard time seeing how his brother could have gone out and sold

18 pairs in just a few hours. The next day, Saturday, the two went off to play their round of golf. Being Saturday, the course was extremely busy. While they were playing, there was some problem ahead on the course. It was causing a big backup delay.

They finally decided to quit after about four holes and walked off the course. It was the first time ever they had walked off a golf course without completing their game. "What are we going to do now," Michael asks his brother. Don says, "Why don't we go sell some more of those shoes and make some money?" Michael says, "No, I don't want to do that". His brother keeps egging him on until Michael gives in. "Alright, I will go, but I am not going into any store." His brother says, "Okay, have it your way." They go back to the store and load up the car with a good variety of sizes and colours. Then, off they go. They pull into a parking lot of a strip mall where there are several stores, including nail and beauty shops, hair salons, and several other small business offices. His brother loads up with several pairs, heads off to the beauty shop, and disappears inside. Michael continues to sit in the car. He keeps telling himself, I am not doing this. I'm not going in. I'm not. After a while, he starts to become bored waiting in the car, so he steps outside to stretch his legs. After pacing around for a few minutes, he makes an executive decision. The car is parked directly in front of a Merle Norman cosmetic store. He can see there are no customers currently in the store. He marshals up his courage, grabs a couple of boxes of shoes, and heads toward the store. He has no sooner walked through the door when the sales lady looks over at him. She smiles as she quickly recognizes the names on the boxes. The boxes themselves are very fancy and very recognizable. Her eyes light up, and she excitedly asks him, "Do you have those shoes inside the boxes?" Before he can answer, she blurts out, "I have a pair, and I am wearing them. I love them." She steps out from behind the counter to show him. Michael nods in the affirmative. Michael hands her one of the boxes of the two he has brought in to show. "How much are they?" she asks. Michael tells her, and she has a big smile. Hearing the price is lower than the retail stores, she is now even more excited. "Do you have this one in red in a size 9?" she asks.

"I am not sure I do, he replies, but let me go check the inventory in the car." He quickly goes back to the car and sorts through the boxes. Aha, he has a red size 9 in the style she wanted. She is delighted when he returns with them. She quickly tries them on and, with her next breath, tells Michael, "I'll take them." Boy, that was the easiest sale ever, he thinks to himself. How did I just do that?

Michael's mind began churning; lights were coming on. She now told him she has many friends who also had them and, at that price, would probably like to get some more. The bells and whistles are going off even more in the young leprechaun's mind. As he heads back to the car, he sees his brother coming out of another store, and his arms are empty. He had sold all that he had taken. He sees Michael almost at the car with the boxes in his arms.

He says to Michael, "You didn't?" Michael holds up the check to show his brother. Don says, "Congratulations, Michael. I told you that you could do it." A very interesting part of the story is Michael had grown up with a stutter. It had been quite the barrier to overcome. Going into an unknown business to sell shoes and being able to talk without the stutter was a major confidence builder. The leprechaun was stepping into a whole new territory. So now Michael sees an opportunity to create a brand-new business for himself and his family.

He couldn't wait to go home, tell his wife about it, and get the show on the road. When his brother has gone home, he tells his wife Margie that he is going to start a new business, a traveling shoe and leather goods store. He tells her if his brother can go out with no experience and sell 18 pairs in an afternoon, and I sell a pair without hardly uttering a word, there is definitely something to be had with this. He tells her that on Monday, he is going to go down to the local dealership and pick out a vehicle for his needs.

First thing Monday morning, he heads down to the truck dealership in Mission Valley, scopes out a truck, and does the basic paperwork. He goes back home and gets Margie so she can drive the car home. While they were at the dealership looking at the truck, Margie kept glancing over at another one. She felt it was better looking. It was a beautiful, extended large van type of vehicle. She told him that she liked the one she was looking at better than the one Michael was showing her. Michael looked over at the one she was pointing at and agreed with her. What he didn't tell her was that he was the one he really wanted. He was hoping she would pick that one, too, and she did.

Below is a picture of the van Michael turned into his traveling leather goods and shoe store. They made a good deal, signed the paperwork, and headed home. The new venture was about to make its start.

Now, Michael had to go to work to outfit the vehicle. He had to create it so it would serve the needs of what he planned to do with it. Michael, utilizing his skill as a carpenter, soon had the vehicle outfitted with a wooden floor covered by thick carpeting. He put in rows of shelves on the front and side walls to carry and display the shoes. He also had six nice chairs for the ladies to sit and try on the new shoes. He built a portable step so his customers could easily and safely able to enter and exit the vehicle. All he needed was to stock the vehicle with shoes, high-quality handbags, and purses to get the show on the road.

He next made a trip up to Los Angeles, where the shoes were manufactured and warehoused. The line of shoes he was going to sell was sold in all the major retail outlets, so they were very well known. He met with the owners and told them what he planned to do. He made a large purchase of many sizes, colours, and styles of shoes. Once he was loaded up, he hit the road back to San Diego. With the vehicle fully stocked and set up, it became a beautiful leather store on wheels. It was loaded with shoes, purses, and other quality leather goods. In the next couple of days, he mapped out his route. He was now ready to start the business. Michael had to tell himself that he must go to a place where there might be a potential customer and not be picky or choosey. Michael told me. When he first started out, he had no real pitch. He would walk into an office with a few boxes, which most women recognized. That was his introduction. After his second visit, he became known as the shoe man. He wasn't Michael, he was now the shoe man. The business was very popular and immediately flourished and prospered. Michael was in the black in very short order. At its height, the business was hitting a grand slam every month and well into the six figures a year. He also started doing the major fairs, and that turned out to be highly successful and profitable as well. The action that really turned out to be a barn buster and really expanded the business was putting on shoe parties at the ladies' homes in the evenings and occasionally on a weekend day. He had been doing his regular route when one of the women at a regular stop asked Michael If he could possibly do a shoe party at her home. Michael thought it over, then told her, yes, he could do that. It soon became another smashing home run. He was soon doing several of these a week and having a grand slam in sales each evening. He never had to ask to look for one as he was always booked up many weeks in advance. This went on like this for four years. At the height of his business, he was hitting daily home runs in sales. Every day was like a great day at the ballpark. Michael would have to make a trip at least once a week, every Monday, to LA and load up on shoes for the following week. The shoe Company was owned by two brothers, whom he came to know quite well. Michael became one of their largest regular customers, so they were always happy to see him each week. There were many styles and many colours of the shoes, and Michael always filled up his van. There was one particular style that sold exceptionally well. Michael decided to see what kind of deal he could get if he purchased 1000 pairs at once.

Nobody buys a thousand pairs of shoes of the same type at one time unless they are a corporate office buying for many store outlets. Michael had in mind a particular price he hoped to get them for. He had brought that amount in cash with him. When Michael brought it up, the brothers were taken a little aback. They told Michael to wait and they would go and figure out a cost for him. They came back with an unbelievable price. It was half of what Michael had hoped for, and Michael was elated but had to force himself to stay calm. They told him to go back to the warehouse and pick out the ones he wanted. He could pick and choose as he desired. He loaded all thousand pairs in his vehicle, paid the invoice, and was off back to San Diego. There, he would sell all thousand pairs in very short order. This business surely met all the happy points, the points that made it a very successful one to own. The leprechaun had surely created another pot of gold for himself and his family. Michael ran this business very successfully for about four years, but the hours were long, and Michael, being the workaholic he is, was starting to burn himself out, but he didn't realize it. Margie was noticing, and under her urging, he went in to see a doctor. The Doctor told him bluntly, for a young man of his age, he had the vitals of a person more than twice his age. He had better start doing something about it, or he would end up having a heart attack.

Believing what the Doctor said, a young Michael, not wanting to leave behind his young family, decided to make a major change. Wow, what a leprechaun. He was willing to give up this wonderful business he created literally from scratch. That was when he made the decision to move out of the state and move to southern Arizona.

He felt if he stayed where he was, he would be drawn back into it. The money he was making would be far too tempting to give up. Michael continued to do the trade show circuit very successfully from his new location but would not be working around the clock as much, at least for a little while.

Michael has always been kind and thoughtful, but do not purposely betray his kindness. You will soon find yourself on the short end of the stick. This next story fully illustrates this point very well.

It was a fall season when he was doing the Fresno Fair in Mid-state California. Michael was selling the shoes at the time. Michael had secured himself the number one corner location in a very high-traffic flow area. It was adjacent to the beer garden stand, a very popular spot. He was busy setting up his booth the day before the start of the fair. He noticed another vendor a couple of booths down the line trying to set up his booth. He was trying to set it up in a tent that had been supplied by the fair. The problem was it wasn't high enough for the setup the fellow had. Michael talked it over with his wife about trading spots with the guy to help him out. She agreed, so he went over to see him. He offered to give the guy his spot as Michael didn't need the height. He told him it wouldn't make a big difference just being a couple of booths over. It wasn't true; it was a Huge Difference, but Michael wanted to help a fellow vendor. He went to the fair manager, who he knew very well, to let him know what was going on.

That way, there would be no upset or confusion for fair management. The vendor was selling cowboy hats. He was very thankful for Michael's offer and took him up on it. Michael did very well with his shoes, but he noticed the guy with the hats was super busy. He had sold most of his inventory after the first weekend of the eighteen-day fair. He would have to drive back to LA and get more stock. This was the time of Urban Cowboy, starring John Travolta. He left a crew looking after the booth while he was gone to LA. Michael asked the guy before he left if he could buy some hats from him. He wouldn't be selling at any shows, just as an add-on to sell at Christmas at his San Diego leather Store. The guy said sure, no problem, and would bring back some for Michael when he returned. The vendor was gone until mid-week. When the hat vendor returned, he brought his wife back with him. He didn't even say hello to Michael. He always seemed to be busy when Michael would look his way. It was getting near the end of the day when Michael thought he had an opening to get the guy's attention. He yelled over, "Did you get me those hats you said you would bring back for me?" Now the guy's wife, who is between them, pipes up in a very loud and rude manner and yells, "Who do you think you are? We are not going to sell you any hats. We are not going to put you in the hat business."

The husband ignores Michael. Well, what do we have here, mused Michael to himself. That was not a good thing to do to someone who went out of their way to help so they could have a successful show.

It felt like getting stabbed in the back. Little did they know, they had made a huge mistake crossing this leprechaun. It would cost them a great deal of money in the future. They had just driven the leprechaun into the hat business. It hadn't been his intention to do so. But it sure was now. It was time for super payback. You will see how it was accomplished as we go through this book.

Michael was fuming. His wife couldn't get him to calm down. He finally sent her home halfway through the show. He ended up finishing the show by himself.

Michael fired off many daggers in their direction before the show came to an end. As mentioned earlier, the manager who ran the Fresno Fair was a friend of Michaels. Before coming to manage the Fresno Fair, he had been the assistant manager of a much larger fair in Del Mar. Michael did that fair on a yearly basis, so he had come to know the manager quite well. Before the fair ended, Michael went to the fair office to talk with his friend; he related to him what had gone down with the vendor he had helped out. The manager told him he should have come and told him what had occurred. Michael said no, he would just like to know that next year, he would like to get his spot back and wouldn't be anywhere near this lying character.

The Manager said not to worry, he would put the vendor out behind a building where his traffic would be very slow. Michael smiled and agreed that would be a good idea. The payback was already in motion. This leprechaun didn't mess around. This was not all. Michael decides he will find out where the guy purchased his hats. Michael will now go into the hat business. He will find out what shows the guy books and will book the same shows where he will be sure to sell the hats at a better price. It will be a great reminder to the guy not to cross a leprechaun. Michael soon had a very successful business selling the hats.

The next year, he called the Del Mar fair and told them he wanted to bring in a new product: cowboy hats. He was told they had granted space to another vendor with cowboy hats. Michael asked what the name of the vendor was. He was told Black Stallion Hats. It was just like rockets had just gone off. It was the same vendor who had betrayed him at the Fresno Fair. Michael tells them what had happened with this vendor in Fresno. As soon as they hear the story, they tell Michael, you are in, he is out. He brought in the hats, and he did extremely well. It was over the top, like a grand slam home run. Just so you know, leprechauns have long memories. They do not forget who abuses them. Just like horses, never forget those who abuse them. It was now 35 years later. Michael and his son were doing the Orange County Fair, selling golf markers and other golf items. Michael decided to go for a walk around to see who was vending at the fair. Some that he hadn't seen for years. He was walking about, and he saw this sign that said Black Stallion

Hats. He thinks to himself, you must be kidding. It is the same guy he had the run-in with at the Fresno Fair about 35 years ago. He walks in and sees even though many years have passed, sure enough, it is the same fellow. Michael walks in and says hello. He then asks the guy; do you remember me? I remember you. The guy looks at Michael with a blank stare and says no, I don't. Michael, for the duration of the fair, walks into the vendor's booth every day. Each time, he asks him if he remembers him now. Each time, he gives a little hint, but the guy never twigs. On the last day, he finally tells him who he is. The guy turns white, his mouth falls open, and his jaw almost hits the ground. Michael knew he had made his point. As we have said many times. Do not cross a leprechaun. Here is another amazing story that will highly influence later happenings down the road.

Michael, in 1984, lands himself a booth near the entrance to the Olympic Summer Games held in Los Angeles. He was selling cowboy hats with red, white, and blue ribbons along with USA pins. Vendors had to pay high prices, four thousand dollars, just to be in the prime traffic spot they had. Many illegal, unlicensed roadside vendors started showing up, clogging the street and blocking off all the legal vendors. Again, they were there illegally, with no license to do business there. The licensed vendors were becoming very upset with what was happening. The vendors told the police. But the police did nothing to enforce the laws. Finally, the vendors had enough. The vendors held a Morning meeting amongst themselves to decide what they were to do about the situation. Michael got up on a standard and told them he was going to go to see the local Police Chief. He was going to see about getting this problem handled pronto. He went down to the station and met with the Chief that evening. He told him if the police didn't take responsibility for handling the vendors by 12 noon the next day, the vendors would start to make citizen arrests of each of the violators. They would confiscate their goods. They would also have the major news outlets and reporters there to see what was taking place. It would be a huge black eye for the Olympics, as well as the city of Los Angeles. The next day, at 8:30 am, police in plain clothes came to Michael's booth. They told him that Mayor Bradley had been woken up in the middle of the night. He was told what the vendors planned to do the next morning. The mayor told the police chief to get it handled immediately. They told Michael they were there to straighten things out. The police Officer told him they would take care of this. He said that the law stated they would have to warn all the illegal vendors first. If they didn't leave, then they could be arrested and removed. Michael told them they had to come to the vendor meeting at 9 am and explain to the other vendors what was going to be done, which they did. As all the unlicensed vendors started showing up, they were told they had to leave. By noon, all the illegal vendors were gone, and the licensed vendors had their space back again. It would have been a PR nightmare if it had hit the papers and television during the Olympics.

The inning was out with no runs in and the vendors went on to win the game. The leprechaun had hit another home run. He was continuing to rack them up on a regular basis. While he was vending there, Michael noticed another vendor a few booths away who had a gigantic booth in the shape of a six-pack of Budweiser, a well-known beer. His booth was always super busy, with several long lineups to its several entrances. Michael went and looked and saw that the vendor was selling beautiful licensed Olympic pins. A few days later, he sees the vendor outside of his tent being interviewed by someone from the press. When the conversation had ended, Michael went up and introduced himself. He tells the pin vendor that he was just down the street from him, selling hats and pins, but nothing as nice as the ones this vendor is selling. This vendor is the only one licensed to sell official Olympic pins through the Olympic Games. The vendor takes a liking to Michael. He invites him into his tent to look. Michael sees there are thousands of pins of all sizes and colours throughout. It is an amazing collection, with prices ranging from a few dollars to a few hundred dollars. He takes Michael back to his office in the booth and asks him if he would like to sell the pins. Michael tells him he doesn't have a lot of cash to outlay for buying a bunch of pins.

The fellow says, "Not to worry, I will give them to you on a consignment basis; just pay me every couple of days for what you sell." He tells Michael he has made a great deal of money at This Olympic Games so far. It was over 2.5 million in the Olympics when they were only halfway through. Michael can't believe the offer he is being given. When he tells his wife, she can't believe it either. The vendor tells Michael he has made so much money in such a short period of time that he is happy to help another hard-working vendor. Michael sells the pins for the last several days of the Olympics. He does extremely well. He ends up making over thirty-five thousand dollars selling these pins. It is a nice golden bonanza for the leprechaun and his wife. This was another grand slam for the leprechaun. Have a look at the hat he wore, pictured here. It has a couple of pounds of pins on it. It is another good story that would demonstrate Michael's ability to overcome adversity and to continue to win at the game he was playing.

Once again, we see the luck of this possible leprechaun. We are going to interject a story because it really shows what it takes sometimes to face up to major challenges and overcome them to the benefit of all concerned.

We will call this segue; "The Time I Strapped Iron on In Quartzsite." This is the story in his own words. I was doing the gem show in Quartzsite, Arizona, a few miles east of the border of California off HWY 10. I had done this show successfully several times prior. We had to check in on Wednesday as the show officially started on Thursday. We arrived in the afternoon, and I went into the office to sign the contract and pay for the space. As I was filling out the contract, the office clerk asked me if I had a dog. She said there was an extra ten-dollar fee if we had a dog. I told her, no, we just have our cat as usual. She then stated we would have to pay ten dollars to have the cat. I told her, I was not paying ten dollars because I had my cat in the RV. It is also not in the contract. She didn't pursue it any further. I finished the paperwork, paid for the space, and then went out to set up my booth. We had the booth set up well before dark and retired for a good night's sleep. I was up early the next morning. I was out, like many other vendors, doing the final touches to be ready for the day's traffic. It was now around 8 am in the morning. The official show opening was at 9 am. I looked down the road between the rows of booths straddling both sides of it. I observed the owner of the land we were set up on striding with determination up the road. *Uh-oh,* I thought to myself, *he is on his way to get in someone's face.* I wouldn't want to be that person.

Now, before I go on with this part of the story, let me backtrack a little and give you a little more background on this character. This guy was not a very amiable type at all. He was, in fact, downright obnoxious. The rumour had it, the year before, we had not seen him because he had been in jail for abusing his wife. Vendors more or less tried to steer clear away from him because of his miserable disposition. He had kicked out and destroyed some vendors' booths in the past because he felt they had somehow violated one or more of his rules. The evening before, when we had come in and set up, he had demanded that all vendors were to show up at a mandatory 10 o'clock meeting. This was so he could let everyone know the rules. He parked his pickup in a big lot in front of us with a couple of his henchmen standing by. He leaned across the hood of his truck with a bullhorn in his hand. He then commenced to give us the lowdown. The first thing he said was, "You have probably heard a bunch of nasty rumours about me. I want you to know they are all true". He then continued, "You all better follow the rules, or you will be kicked out immediately, and you will not get your money back."

Now, this guy in the past had literally come along with a backhoe and destroyed some vendor's booth because of some assumed misdeed in this guy's eyes.

That was our welcome and greeting to start off the show. Friendly welcome, wouldn't you say?

Now, back to the next morning. I see him come striding up the road in my direction with a couple of his henchmen. He comes to an abrupt stop in front of my booth. Without a hello, he barks, "Do you have a cat here?" "Yes, I reply, I have my cat here every year." "Well, now you are out of here," he retorts. "You have an hour to get it together and get gone, or I will be back with the backhoe, and I will rip you out of here. You now have 59 minutes," he barks as he turns and abruptly stomps off. Well, now, this was truly a dilemma. There was no way I could tear down and be out of there in one hour. I had to decide what to do and do it fast. I was also not going to let him come and bulldoze my booth and endanger my wife and boys. He had done this to others in the past. I had a gun in my RV, but what was this leprechaun supposed to do?

My vendor neighbours had seen and heard what had gone on. When he left, they started coming over to my booth. Most were older couples semi-retired. They were just out to make a few extra dollars. They were all concerned about my present situation. "What are you going to do Michael?" I was asked. "I am not sure, I replied, but there is no way I am going to let him put my family and livelihood in danger." We can all help back you up. Several of them volunteered. We have guns in our RVs. WOW, now I already had a posse.

I thanked each for their offers. I had decided I needed to call the local town sheriff and get him involved quickly. Back in those days, there were no cell phones. There were only payphones. There were only two of them available in the whole darn town. One happened to be on the property where we were renting our space. Because of this scarcity of phones, there were always long lineups of vendors waiting to use them. I quickly walked over to the one on a pole by the gate. There were at least thirty people lined up waiting to use it. I quickly walked up to the lady who was currently on it and stated loudly," I need to use that phone right now, it could be a matter of life and death." She immediately hung up and handed me the phone. There were scowls and looks of curiosity from the rest of the vendors that were waiting. I soon had the sheriff's office on the line. My opening line was, "I need to speak to the sheriff. He needs to get his ass over to this location now, or somebody is likely to get shot. There was a slight silent pause on the other end, and then, "Sheriff, you need to take this call." The sheriff quickly comes on the line and says, "What's this about a shooting? Who is going to shoot who?" I replied, "I am going to be doing the shooting if you do not get over here now." I gave him my name and booth space. Before I hung up the phone, he cautioned me not to do any shooting before he got there. There were many open mouths looking my way as I headed off back to my booth. I quickly arrived back at my setup to wait for the sheriff to show up. I must admit he was quick. Just as I get back to my booth, I see him striding down the road towards me. He doesn't look very happy.

He stops in front of me and then asks, "Are you the one who just called me? What is going on?"

"Yes, I am," I replied and quickly related to him what had happened. I then asked him if it was in my right to pack a gun. Could I shoot the guy if I felt my and my family's lives were in danger? He tells me yes, but he doesn't want things to go that far. I can see he is quite upset about the whole situation. He tells me this has happened before with this guy. He had told him to knock it off. He asked me to wait at my booth. He will go and talk to the guy and come back to tell me what is going to go down. In another twenty minutes, I can see him heading back up the road towards me. "Okay," he states, "You can have all day to move out. He won't bother you, but if he does, get hold of me before you start shooting". With that, he walks off, shaking his head and mumbling to himself.

Well, I am not happy, but at least I hope I won't have to shoot anyone. I go in the camper, get my gun and strap it on. I still don't know what this guy might try or do. I am not ready to trust him at this time. I tell my wife we will have to take down the booth and leave. I tell her not to hurry as we have all day. Since I have paid for this spot, we will use it as long as we can.

It is about 10 in the morning now. I see him, the landowner, walking up towards me. He is alone this time. He doesn't have any of his henchmen with him. I see him eyeing to where I have my gun strapped on my hip. He stops just outside my booth space, where he just stands and watches to see what we are doing. After a while, I began thinking to myself, I wonder if anyone ever stood up to this bully, man to man. I wondered if anyone had ever had a face-to-face talk with him. With that thought in mind, I walked over to him and stood facing him. I point blank ask him. "Has anyone ever talked to you man to man?" He looks a little confused like this is a completely new thought to him. There is a very long pause." No, he finally says, no, no one has." "Well, I say, I would like to talk with you man to man. Can we do that?" Again, there is a long pause. Finally, he responds, "Yeah, I guess we could do that." I tell him, "Good, let's go over behind the booth by the RV where we can have a man-to-man talk." I head over to the camper truck, and he follows me. When we are away from everyone, I ask him. "Have I ever been a problem to you in all the previous times I have come here?" He thinks for a while, then slowly replies. "No, no, you haven't." "Okay, I tell him. "Now, I want you to put yourself in my shoes. If I am running this place and you come here. I change the rules, and I want you to pay more money you didn't expect to pay. Might you be a little upset?" Again, there is a long pause and then his reply. "Why yes, I guess I would be." So I say to him, "Well, good then, so you can see why I might not want to pay extra for my cat this year." The pause was less this time. His answer was a little quicker, "Yea, I guess I can see you have a point there". There was another long pause and then he said, "You know, I am going to give you your money back. I have never done that before." I thank him for that and then say to him, "You know what might be a better solution? You keep the money. Since I am already set up, I will just stay and finish the show. We can just forget what happened earlier."

There is another lag in his response, then a smile breaks the seriousness of his face. He originates. "Yea that's a good idea." We shook on it, and he left. It would seem that no one had ever taken the time to have real communication with this guy before. The funny part of this story is that every day of the show, after we had our talk, he would walk up to my booth, smile and hail me, "Hi Michael, how are you doing? Hope you are having a great show."

Needless to say, I had several surprised neighbours. It is a kind of funny story to look back on, but at the time, it didn't seem so funny. I was proud of how I handled it. We all won. We had a successful event, and no one was shot! The leprechaun had pulled off another one. Another home run. That is really the way it went down, believe it or not. It is amazing how far a little communication will take a non-optimum situation and bring about a positive resolution. It was after this show with Quartzsite still in their rear-view Mirror Michael originates to Margie, he is going to start a new business, selling pins. She looks at him with a bit of a puzzled expression. She tells him the pin business is dead. He replies, "I know but I am going to revive it." This he surely does indeed. More to come on this subject.

Now, being on the road a good deal of the time, some very strange things can happen. One year, Michael and his family travelled to Cheyenne, Wyoming, to do Frontier Days. It is a huge outdoor western rodeo. It is a very big tourist attraction. It is well attended by people from all over the world. Michael was selling cowboy hats and pins. It's a very good venue. They, of course, did very well, as usual. From there, they are headed south to the Fort Collins Rodeo in Colorado. There were a few days before the next show was to begin, so they decided to make a short vacation of it. They visit Estes Park, where Michael buys a fishing license in a small town called Deer Ridge Junction on the other side of the mountain from the park. It would be good to have in case they were able to do some fishing. They spend two days in the town but don't have an opportunity to do any fishing. When they are leaving, Michael goes to the ranger and lets him know they are leaving. Michael asks if he can change the dates on the fishing license. They have not used it but might have an opportunity on their way south. The ranger is happy to oblige. He writes in the changes and initials them. This is important, as you will see shortly. The family goes back to Este Park. When they leave Estes Park, they head south towards Fort Collins. It is late afternoon when Michael spots an area where he can get off the highway. It is just along the side of a river. Since it is near dinner time, he decides to pull off and get something to eat. Once parked, he starts pulling things out of the camper on the back of the truck. The boys, in the meantime, had gone down to the river to check it out. There are several fishing poles which he stands up leaning on the side of the vehicle. It is only a few minutes later when a park ranger pickup pulls in and parks behind him. The ranger walks up, looks at the poles and says, "Doing some fishing?" Michael tells him, "No, but he does have a license in case he does decide to fish." Although he doesn't have to be on the up and up, he decides to show the ranger his license. This turned out to be the wrong thing to do. The ranger looks it over and then says, "You changed it." Michael tells him, no, the ranger at Deer Ridge Junction changed it. You can see where he initialled it. You can call him and verify it." The ranger tells him again, "You changed it. I am going to have to arrest you and take you in. I must charge you for altering a legal government document. It was now starting to get dark out. Michael's family were out in the middle of nowhere. He was starting to become irate as this official was being a very anal, uncaring and unthinking individual. Michael went over to Margie and filled her in on what was happening. He told her he shouldn't be long. He told her and the boys to stay near the vehicle until he returned. He gets in the pickup with the ranger, and they head back down the highway the way they had just travelled. Michael, not in a very gentle way, berated the park official all the way to his office. He kept telling him to call the other ranger and this could all be straightened out now. The fellow would have none of it. For whatever reason, this fellow would not listen. They get to his office, and the paperwork is filled out. He then tells Michael that he has to take him to the local Police station to have him booked, which is in Estes Park.

Michael is really becoming exasperated now. It is fully dark out. His family is out in the middle of nowhere and does not know what is going on. Michael tells him they will have to stop and let his family know what is occurring, or he will get him charged with family endangerment. This seemed to sink in somewhat in the ranger's thick head and he agreed. When they get back to the camper Michael quickly fills them in. He tells them he will get this sorted out and be back as quickly as he can. Amen

They drive to the police station and Michael continues to berate this wooden head until they arrive. As they get out of the vehicle, a very brisk breeze was blowing. The ranger's briefcase opens and all the papers spill out and start blowing helter-skelter in all directions. He frantically runs after each piece, trying to grab it up before it is blown out of reach. Michael laughs out loud and tells him." I hope you don't think I will be helping you to pick them up. After several minutes, he gets the last piece retrieved, and they go into the police station.

The ranger is recognized by the officer at the front desk. The ranger tells him he is here to book me for falsifying a government document. We get the paperwork done. Michael is scheduled to go before a judge in a couple of days in Loveland. I tell the desk sergeant the fact that he hauled me down there, leaving my wife and kids back along the highway by themselves. The sergeant tells the ranger he is to get me back there now. Michael again berated this so-called ranger all the way back to his camper. When he arrives back Michael explains to Margie and his boys the situation. He tells them they will have to hang around for a couple of days for the court appearance. He tells the ranger, I will be glad to see you in court, you had better be there. The ranger did not show up. In two days, Michael shows up at the court and goes into register to find out what time he goes before a judge. While he is waiting in the courtroom, a clerk comes in and asks if anyone wants to see the prosecutor before they go before the judge. Michael decides, yes, he would like to talk to a prosecutor. He is led into another room, where he is introduced to the prosecutor, who asks him what he wishes to discuss. Michael tells him the circumstances of how he ended up here. The prosecutor becomes quite angry after Michael has related his story. We have told this ranger to stop doing this nonsense, or we are going to charge him. He has pulled this stunt on others who were traveling through the state. The prosecutor gets all the data and tells Michael this case is dismissed. Michael is told he is free to go and gets an apology for the treatment he and his family have received from an official in the state of Colorado. They drive to the next event, where they are soon set up; Michael gets into a conversation with his neighbouring vendor, a taxidermist. Michael relates to him about his recent experience in Colorado with the ranger. "Oh, that guy, I know him well," his fellow vendor says, "I have had several run-ins with that fellow. Here is some good news on that subject, which might make you feel a little better". Apparently, this ranger had been harassing some local ranchers. They were thoroughly fed up with him and his tactics. One late night, they went to his house. They grabbed him up and took him down a dark country road for several miles. There. They stripped him of all his clothes and left him there to walk back home totally naked. They gave him a warning to knock it off, or much worse things could happen to him the next time they saw him. That made Michael feel a little better. It certainly hadn't been one of the best experiences that Michael had, but he did come out of it as a leprechaun should. There was some justice and retribution, after all. A little hard to believe, but it's a true story. Just another day in the life of a possible leprechaun.

Michael, as you will read in the chapter, the Horse Whisperer became involved in the quarter horse business, where he bred, showed, trained and sold horses. It was a very rewarding but a very expensive business to be in. At one point, Michael was maintaining forty-plus horses on his property. To finance his operation at this level, he needed a regular source of income. As we mentioned earlier, he decided to go back into the pin business. His wife was somewhat sceptical, but she knew there was no use arguing with him once he made up his mind. He was going to give it his best. He methodically set out to create it to be a success. He made up a number of attractive display stands and filled them with pins he felt would be popular and would sell well. He spent the next two weeks in the Tucson area, pitching to many different shops around the city, but didn't even make one sale. Michael was not a quitter. He was sure he was not barking up the wrong tree. He decided he was going to take the show on the road to see how he would fare. He had never done anything like this before, but he honestly believed he still could make it a success. He told Margie he was going to be gone for a couple of weeks to see what he could do with this venture on the road. He started hitting all the truck stops along the major highways in Arizona as well as all types of gift and convenience stores in all the small towns he would travel through. There are many, many of them along the highways and the byways throughout the state. He would make notes after each presentation. What was successful or unsuccessful until he condensed it down to a simple, one-page presentation. That became the total spiel he used to close his sales. He was soon making a sale in almost every stop he made. He would tell his new customers that he would be back around once a month to fill the stand with brand-new pins and take out the old ones that weren't selling. That way, they would not get stuck with a product that was not moving. Again, he was applying his four steps that needed to be in to ensure it was successful and all were happy. He soon had many men and outlets moving his merchandise. He continued to build up his route and soon was going as far east as Tennessee and out to the Pacific shores of California. He was consistently hitting home runs daily. He was making more than enough to carry and finance his horse business. He found the supplier for the best selection of quality pins and stocked only the bestsellers. Michael was always the number one buyer and seller for his supplier and who of course was always very happy to see Michael when he came to reorder. His supplier didn't always have the ones Michael wanted and he would continually ask for them. Michael later found an even bigger supplier in Houston, Texas so he was able to expand his line of successful selling pins.

Michael, as he tended to do, pushed himself to the point where his body would just give out on him. Because of how the business was, Michael could do the business pretty much twenty-four hours a day, which he did a good deal of the time. He didn't eat well and, he was not getting the rest he needed. Here is another instance where he was saved from death, whether from being the leprechaun or because he had someone watching his back. Most likely, a combination of both.

He was somewhere down in the southeast, servicing his route. He was as usual, putting in his typical 18 hours plus day. He was driving along pretty much exhausted. He pulls into a truck stop just inside the Arkansas border, along I-40, to take a shower and refresh himself. Afterwards, he feels so much better. He thinks to himself, now I can keep on going for the rest of the day. He decides to keep on going. He has been driving 70 miles an hour for most of the last couple of days going down the highways. This is where God comes in to save this leprechaun once more. Five miles down the road, part of a 5000-mile trip so far travelled, he is coming up to a quarter-mile section where there happens to be a Highway Patrol Inspection Station. There is only one lane going into the station off the main section of the highway. You have to slow down to thirty- five mph. As Michael slows down on this section, in an instant, he starts to fade out. It was like his battery had suddenly gone dead. He thinks to himself, what the heck is happening? Am I dying? The last thing he remembers saying aloud, "OH Lord, don't let me die in Arkansas. He did not go to sleep; his body just quit, and he blacked out. His vehicle slowly rolls off the road into the median and comes to a gentle stop. He was out for some time. The next thing he is aware of is he is very slowly coming to and wondering if he had, in fact, died.

No, he is in his vehicle down in the lower median between the highways. He finds it almost impossible to operate the body. He sees he has come to a stop less than 100 feet from the DOT Inspection Station. After some minutes have passed, he is finally able to control his body well enough to drive his vehicle out of the ditch and to the east side of the highway. He parks the vehicle next to the station office. He slowly gets out of the van and, in a very wobbly manner, walks to the station, where an inspection officer opens the door and tells him to come in and sit down. She says she saw him drive off the road. She asks him what happened. He told her he didn't know. She was wondering if she should call for an ambulance. She asks him if he is okay and if he should call an ambulance. Michael figures it might be a good idea, so she goes ahead and calls for one. The paramedics arrived shortly to take his vitals. They question him about what happened. Michael explains the scenario that led up to him passing out. The paramedics tell him he just passed out from sheer exhaustion. He needed to get a room and get some very much-needed sleep. He also needed to eat something as he hadn't been eating well.

Michael of course, was very relieved. He thanks the Paramedics. He calls his wife to let her know the situation. She tells Michael to get a room and stay there until he is fully rested. This time, Michael fully complies with his wife's wishes. After getting a good sleep and something to eat, the leprechaun was once again ready to hit the road. He made sure for the rest of the trip home that he did not allow himself to get into any further situations like what had just occurred.

He arrived home safe and sound. Another successful trip was now behind him.

Wow, the leprechaun has another escape from the yawning jaws of death and lives to tell about it. During his travels in Arizona on his route, he met several vendors who watched and saw the success Michael was having. There was a truck stop manager, a novelty vendor, as well as a very good friend, who asked him how they might be able to get into the business. All three of them approached him in the same time period. Michael saw this as an opportunity to help others and to expand. He would wholesale to them and would help them set up their business successfully. Michael would take each one out for two weeks, train, and help them set up their routes with them to help ensure their success. All they had to do to maintain their success was service and work to expand their routes once a month. They needed to follow Michael's successful actions. He helped to set up three new Distributors. Each one soon had a thriving business. He showed each of them how to do the presentations and close a sale almost every time. Everyone seemed to be happy and were soon successfully earning a good living for themselves and their families.

Michael would have the mall meet once a month at his place. He would go over what was selling well and give any help that was needed to ensure their businesses kept growing. It was about six months down the road, and Michael got a call. It was the day before their regular meeting. It was one of his dealers asking if they could meet at a location about 80 miles north of Tucson. This was an unusual request. The leprechaun's warning antenna went up immediately. He knew there was something going on. It probably wasn't a good thing. He told him no, come down to my place and we will meet as usual. When they had all arrived and were seated, Michael asked, "So what's up guys?"

They all sat there with sheepish looks. Finally, one spoke up. We have decided we don't need you anymore he finally blurted out. We have found out where the main supplier is located, and we can get a better price. We know you have been fair, but you know, it's just business. Inside, Michael was furious but kept his head and put on a calm outward appearance. This is not the agreement we made when I set you up in this business, Michael told them. "We know," one replied, "it's just that we got a better deal for us." They had lied to the supplier and had not told him it was Michael who had set them up. He tells them, "I did not set you up in business to make you into my competitors. So, suit yourself. But do so at your own peril. Just remember, I put you in business so I can take you out just as easily." "You wouldn't do that, would you??" one of them asked, "I have a family and bills to pay." "You should have thought of that before you went behind my back," Michael retorted.

After they had left, Michael decided to teach them all a lesson. He knew their routes since he had helped set them up in the first place. He went and bought a bunch of pins that would never sell well. A week before they would start their monthly tour, Michael set out to do their routes. He would go into each location to see what had sold and what still remained. He would replace the stand with the ones that would not sell well, if at all. Sometimes, the store manager would ask what he was doing there. Michael would tell him he was doing the route and was just helping his associate out. He did this store after store until each store had all the stands replaced with pins that would be poor sellers or wouldn't sell. Michael often wished he could have been a fly on the wall each time one of them walked into one of their stores to restock. They would see that what was there was not what they had put. Somewhere along the line, they would realize what had taken place. Michael did this to all three of them until they all knew how they had been outmaneuvered. He did this all in 30 days. In a very short period, about three months, all three were no longer in the pin business. Just one time through their routes was all it took to accomplish the leprechaun's objective. Once again, Michael showed that you do not try to steal a leprechaun's pot of gold. Not when he was helping you get your own pot of gold. You may live to regret it. Believe it or not.

While he was still in the pin business, his California supplier asked Michael if he could come out to Atlanta to see if he could help him collect some money that was owed to him. Michael knew this fellow very well and they had become friends over the years. Apparently, this supplier had given some vendor out in Atlanta a large amount of product on a consignment basis to sell at the 1996 Summer Olympic Games that year. The fellow he had given the product to was not paying him as promised. So, he asked Michael if he would come out to find out what was going on and help collect some of the money owed. Michael agreed to help this supplier friend, so off to Atlanta, Michael goes.

When he arrived there, he found out the vendor had set up many locations and was collecting money but not paying his friend from LA. This was now to the tune of tens of thousands of dollars. Michael first met with the supplier. Michael then met with the fellow who was not paying. He found out the guy was not going to pay for the product he had already sold. So right then, Michael took all of the remaining product back immediately so his friend could cut down his losses.

Michael had taken some of his own products with him so he could possibly make some money for himself during the time he was there. He contacts a vendor who has Olympic vending locations throughout Atlanta. One morning, he was waiting at a warehouse to meet this vendor he had an appointment with. He hears two people coming through the door. He hears the voice of one of them and recognizes it as it is a bit unusual. It is a fellow from California who has known the business for quite a few years earlier. Michael asks him what he is doing there. The fellow says it is all because of you, Michael. It turns out he had listened to Michael about the 84 Olympics in LA. He said Michael had told him how well the vendor who had Olympic pins at those Olympic Games had done. He was so excited about the idea that he had come out to Atlanta two years before the games were to take place. He had secured the exclusive rights for all the licensed Olympic pin sales for the 1996 Olympic Games in Atlanta. He introduced Michael to the fellow Michael was to meet who was looking for other pins to buy. He tells Michael the guy is okay. He has had dealings with him for some time.

Michael sold him about $10,000 of goods, which he paid for by check. When Michael went to cash it, the money was not there, and the guy was in the wind. The check happened to be a two-party check with two signatures on it. He could not track down the one who took the product. The other signer he found out was the top administrator of the biggest hospital in the city of Atlanta. Michael was tired and not in good spirits when he went to see this person to get the check made good. He thought of taking his gun but thought better of it in his current state of mind. There was so much stress on Michael that he even called his wife and told her he might not be coming home. He was very frustrated and tired but determined to get his money back. Michael entered the office building and took the elevator to the 11th floor, where this signer had his office.

He walked up to the receptionist's desk and asked if the fellow was in. She said yes, down the hall, the second door on the left. She asked Michael if he had an appointment. He told her no. She then told Michael he would have to make one. Michael ignores her and heads down the hall. She yells after him, "You can't go in there."

Michael opens the door and walks in. The fellow had a startled look on his face. He asks Michael, who are you, and what do you want? Michael hands the guy the check. He asks, "Is that your signature on there?" The guy looks and says yes. He looks very flustered. He then commences to tell Michael the signature of the other guy is someone who burned him and several of his friends for a large amount of money. After the guy has told his sad sob story, Michael believes what the guy has told him. In fact, he is not going to get the check made good any time soon, or ever.

When he walked out of that office, he felt bad for himself but also felt bad for the other guy. What a leprechaun, he never looked back. It's an unusual way to end a game. The leprechaun may have lost an inning, but the game was far from over. He next called the friend who had obtained the license for the Olympic pins for the Atlanta games. When his friend hears what happened, he is upset. He feels somewhat responsible for getting Michael ripped off. He had told Michael the guy was okay to deal with.

He tells Michael to come over to his house because he wishes to show him something. Maybe he can help him out and help him recoup some of his losses. When he arrives at the house, the guy takes Michael in through the garage. He notices there are rows and rows of shelves, and the shelves are piled high with boxes and boxes of pins. This is repeated as he shows Michael throughout the house. This is like a déjà vu of the Olympic games of Los Angeles 12 years before. He tells Michael to pick out as many pins as he wants and take them on consignment. He can pay for them as he sells them. He wants to help Michael make up for the loss of the 10k. Michael is very thankful. He picks out the pins he feels will sell well. He decides to go to Athens, Georgia, where the Olympic soccer championship games are being played. He finds out what the two teams are playing that day. He loads up on lots of pins and flags for the two countries playing. He acquires the flags from his friend, whom he had initially come out to recover them. He makes up a flat plate to wear on his chest with arms extending out from each side. This he hangs from his neck. On one side, he has pins and flags of one country being represented. On the other side, the other team pins and flags. He is stocked and heads out of the playing field. He sets himself off to the side of the main entrance. He is no sooner there than a security officer shows up and tells him he can't be at that location. Michael asks him where he could stand. The officer points just across the street to where a stairway leads up and down from the stadium. Michael looks and sees people coming down the stairs. Do you mean that spot he points and asks the security person? Yes, he is told, that is fine there. Michael is elated. It is a perfect spot. He walks over and stands at the bottom of the stairs. It was an extremely high-traffic location.

He was no sooner there than he was being bombarded by fans and buyers walking up and making purchases. In very short order, Michael is making sales hand over fist. He is even able to trade for a ticket to go into the stands to watch the event. When he goes into the stadium, he sees that the main supporters for the two teams are mainly set up in two different sections. Michael walks down into the lower stands to where he is below the main spectators. Then he walks across in front of one team's supporters with that country's pins and flags showing. He starts getting orders yelled down to him. In short order, he has sold all the flags and pins for that country's team. He then does the same in front of the other team supporters with repeat results. It was a great day at the games. He sold all his goods and was able to watch the game as well. Michael continued this routine every day of the games, where teams from many different countries competed against each other. Each time, he would sell out his stock, get a ticket to the game, and go home with several thousand dollars in his pockets. It was a very successful venture indeed. Home runs were occurring every day. The leprechaun was back on top as usual. Michael had recouped his losses and made a bundle as well. The soccer games ended, but there were still a couple of days left in the Olympics. Michael wandered to a downtown area of Athens where many other vendors had set up. Michael decided to set up a table close by and sell his wares. He is no sooner set up than a police officer comes by. He says he can't set up there. He needs to have a license to do so. Michael folds up his table and walks down past the vendors. He notices a lady set up who is selling USA Olympic pins, not of the quality of the pins he has. He gets an idea. He walks over to her and starts a quick conversation. He admires her pins and then shows her the pin she has. She immediately recognizes that he has superior-quality pins to sell. Michael then makes her a business proposition. If she allows him to set up and sell his pins at her booth, he will split the profits with her at the end of the day. She quickly agrees, and a new partnership is formed. The pins are selling like hotcakes. The next thing you know, the same Police Officer sees Michael behind the counter with the vendor. He comes over and says to Michael, "I thought I told you that you need a license to set up here." His new partner quickly steps in and says to the officer, "he is my new partner." "Then I guess that's okay, he says. "Michael, to be on his good side, asks him if he could watch over the two of them when they are going to tally up at the end of the day. The officer, being a friend of the vendor, agrees to do so. The situation was fully handled.

Michael was now able to increase his profits even more for his trip. The leprechaun hits another home run.

By the time the games were finished, Michael had recouped his losses and was very much in the black. His trip to the Olympics had turned out on a positive note. He had helped a good friend, and he had been personally rewarded himself. It just goes to show that you never know where good fortune will appear when you are of good heart and are willing to help others along your path through life. That is especially true if you are a leprechaun. Michael was able to do the pin business successfully for many years. It would give a steady cash flow that helped support his horse business, which itself was a major entrepreneurial undertaking. The pin business started out from the idea that it was a dead business, but he revived it to the point where the Leprechaun was making continuing pots of gold.

About eight years or so back, his son Patrick asked him if he would set up a business for him. Patrick was tired of the farrier business as it was very physically demanding. The hard part was dealing with people who thought they knew best. It was very frustrating. Michael was glad to do so. He set him up in a personalized golf marker business. Patrick became very successful at it, doing fairs and other venues throughout California. It was a lot of work, but he made good money. It helped him to be able to do what he really wanted to do. When an opportunity came up to do something, he asked Michael if it would be okay to give the business back to him. Michael said sure. He then turned around and set it up at a very large marketplace in central Arizona. Michael is still running it today. It is, of course, very successful. He sells all kinds of golf-related items and a huge selection of baseball caps, especially for the military personnel who have served their country. He always gives them a very good discount, and they are very appreciative. Going on 80, this leprechaun is still working on creating another pot of gold. He is still hitting the home runs.

Michael—The Horse Whisperer

The definition of a horse whisperer, according to Google, "is a horse trainer who adopts a more sympathetic view with the horse. This is a totally inadequate definition of what a true horse whisperer is all about. A horse whisperer has a much deeper and completely empathetic view of the motives, needs and desires of the horse that he is dealing with. Michael, as a true horse whisper, gets into the mind of the horse and gets the horse's trust to such a degree the horse knows exactly what it is being asked to do. The secret is putting the horse in a classroom situation where it knows it is in a class. The horse fully duplicates and understands at the end of the lesson, what it needs to do, to do it again and again every time it is asked for. The horse on a gradient, given a series of cues which it duplicates and understands what it is being asked to do. As a horse whisperer one needs to recognize all the little mannerisms the horse displays, what they mean and how to correctly deal with them. Michael is definitely a master of these skills. His certainty in his abilities is without question. He is a horse whisperer in the fullest sense.

There are four main points that are his basis of operation: One, he does not get hurt; two, the horse does not get hurt; three, the horse is taught something and learns from the experience; and four, the horse stays calm. If the horse feels safe and understands, the horse will remain calm. Michael's journey from being horseless to a master horse whisperer is one worth telling.

His first encounter with a horse occurred when he was very young. He liked horses and watched lots of cowboy shows on TV. He thought horses were very cool and thought it would be great to have one. However, he didn't have any grand ideas about a life completely involved with them. Michael had an opportunity to go for a ride on one when he was very young by himself. It was both thrilling and very scary. The horse he was on the back of got spooked and took off at a full gallop, with Michael holding on for dear life. The horse galloped down a very steep incline at the same rapid pace. Michael continued to hold on for as hard as he could and amazingly, did not fall off. It had been a real adrenalin rush indeed. Possibly it was because he was a leprechaun that he stayed on the horse.

The next major encounter he had with horses was in his early twenties. Michael had just finished a Bob Cummings leadership course. He had sunk every available extra bit of cash to do the Vitamin business startup. The business was, unfortunately, before its time. The world was not quite ready for this type of business. He told me the course he did in San Francisco was well worth every penny. Michael told me that after getting through that leadership course alive and graduating, he knew that he could accomplish anything he really set out to do. It was a completely life-altering experience for him. It proved to be the case for the rest of his life. At the graduation, each participant received a silver genie lamp. This was very appropriate for a leprechaun. It is a reminder that once you get the genie out of the lamp, do not try to put it back in. That is one thing Michael made sure he never did. Michael felt that the course he did was equal to completing a master's degree in just a few days.

After the course, life was a little rough. He and Margie lived on bread and potatoes and their sons survived on watered-down baby food. The next pot of gold was not far from the horizon. Michael had not had an opportunity to start working at the time, so there was no operating cash on hand. He had invested all their savings into the vitamin business. He had a wife and two young sons to look after. From their past purchases, they had accumulated books of S&H Green and Blue Chip Stamps. They had a big stack of these saved up at the time. These could be redeemed for more products or for cash at a reduced rate. They didn't need products, they needed food, so they opted for cash, which turned out to be about sixty dollars. He talked it over with Margie about what to buy or do with the money. He could take the sixty and buy some food, but then they would be without money again.

It so happened that there was a horse racing track, Hollywood Park, some miles away. He could go and see if he could win enough to double their stake. There was a risk they could end up with less or none. The more that Michael looked at it, the more favour he had for the idea to go to the racetrack. Margie was not quite so sure about it. It seemed a little too risky to her. Michael decided he would take the chance and play the horses. He had a leprechaun feeling he could possibly win and increase his stake. He headed off to the Hollywood Park racetrack well before it would open for the day's races. He purchased a daily racing form and sat down at a bench under a tree in the parking lot. He now began to study it with the idea of picking some of the winning horses running that day. Now don't forget Michael has just finished the life-changing leadership course in San Francisco. While he was sitting there, another man came over and asked if it was okay to sit down beside him to wait for the gates to open. Michael said sure, as he continued going over the daily racing form. The other gentleman would occasionally ask Michael what horses he thought might be good to bet on in a particular race.

Michael would tell him what he thought and then go back to studying the form. When the gates finally opened, they both walked inside and sat down on the concrete base of an upright support by the stairs. It jetted out enough so the two of them could sit. They had not paid to go up into the stands. By this time, Michael had finished studying the racing form for the first couple of races. He was now ready to place his first bet. He went and placed a two-dollar bet on the winning place and show for the first race. He picked it right and won about twelve dollars. That had turned out well. Now he was playing with his winnings. He still had his original purse. He continued his streak for the next couple of races. He either won or had a second-place finisher. His luck and ability to pick the winners was paying off. Like it should, for a leprechaun. At this time there were these relatively new bets now made available at the track. One of them was called an exacta. Each was a minimum five-dollar bet. It was available for the fourth and ninth races only. Here, you could pick the winner and runner-up. If you were able to call them in the right order, depending on their odds, the payout could be very lucrative. Now it is the fourth race.

Michael decided to go for it. He picked out the key horse, Turbulator, the number one favourite he felt would win. It had 1 to 10 odds. He picked two horses to come in second. One had 44 to 1 odds. He was the number 7 horse called Flying Magician. The second backup horse was at 12 to 1. The key horse went off at 1 to 5. He had seen something about the runner-up horse on the racing form that made him think the 44 to 1 was a much better horse than the odds makers had put him at. That horse had only raced two times, but had a first and second place. It had not raced in over a year. All the other horses had many races under them but were not in the money. Michael made two, five-dollar bets on the exacta and a couple of two-dollar bets on place and show. Michael was very nervous about this race. Picking the winners of this race would immediately and greatly improve his financial situation. Michael couldn't stand sitting there, just waiting for the race to start. He gets up and walks down beside the track to the final turn before the home stretch. The race is on and Michael waits for the horses to come around the final turn. As they finally come around the bend, he sees that the favourite is well out in front by himself. The rest of the field is pretty much bunched up. As they come around the turn at the top of the stretch, the first horse he sees is the number 6 horse in second place. It is not a long shot. Now he sees another horse making its move. It's coming up quickly down along the rail and is about to take over 2nd place. It is the long shot he picked. Michael is now starting to get very excited but still very nervous, as the race is not over.

All he sees is the rears of the horses as they race toward the finish line. He starts heading back down towards the finish line in front of the grandstands. Michael knew the favourite had won easily and was praying his long shot had come in second. As he gets to the Grandstands, before he can see the board, he hears the announcer give the results. WOW, he had done it. He has picked his horses correctly. The fellow that came in with him was still sitting where he had left him. He had seen Michael cash in winning tickets of the earlier races. He tells Michael as he walks up, "You know some long shot came in second."

"I know," Michael tells him. "Look at the racing form. That is the one you pointed out to me", he replies. The fellow looks at him and asks, "Did you bet on it?" Michael nods and the fellow says, "Boy that will pay." At the same time, the results were shown on the big board.

Michael had won over 600 for his bets on that race. The other fellow had lost out as he did not follow Michael's lead. Michael has now, in four races, picked three winners and one second. This was becoming very exciting; the trip to the track was paying him big dividends. Michael continued to pick firsts and seconds up to the last race of the day. The last race was the second exacta. Michael now had more confidence in likely picking the top horses in the final race. Michael again picked three horses for this last race. One to win and either of the two others to come in second. The horse that Michael picked twin was one of the favourites. The horses he picked to come in second went off at odds of about 15 to one. He bet a total of ten dollars. Michael, this time, went up in the stands right in front of the finish line, where he would hopefully see some very exciting results. His winning pick came in all by himself well out in front. There were three horses running for the second-place finish just back of the leader. They were all running in a straight line across.

Just before they reached the finish line, the middle horse dropped back. The two outside, which Michael had picked, crossed in a photo finish. It was too close to tell who came in second. Either way, he would win. Both horses were around the same odds, so either way, he would do very well. When the official announcement came over the loudspeaker, his pick had indeed come in second. He had won well over 300 in that race. His new friend asked him wistfully, "Did you have the winners there too?"

"Yes, I had all three," Michael replied.

"Boy you made some good money today," the fellow said, with a little sadness in his voice. The poor fellow didn't listen to his new leprechaun friend. If he had done so, he too could have had pockets full of cash, his own pot of gold. It was a totally leprechaun kind of day, to say the least. This definitely wasn't the typical day at the racetrack. Michael was blessed to pick winner after winner. The day at the track had turned his initial 60 into over 1300, an excellent day's winnings. He was excited to go home and surprise Margie with the spoils of his great day at the races. Michael had hit two grands lams out of the park in the same game. His pockets now full of cash, Michael headed across the parking lot of the racetrack to his vehicle so he could go home and surprise Margie. As he is walking across the parking lot, he notices a group of individuals in the middle of the lot huddled in a circle. Michael, being curious, walks over to see what is going on. He quickly observed that they were playing a betting game called Three Card Monte. After a couple of minutes of seeing how it was going, he pulls out a hundred-dollar bill from his horse race winnings. He starts to put it in the pot. As he bends over to place his bet, the bill is snatched from his fingers. He couldn't see who had taken it as his view was cut off by the crowd behind him. He quickly gets out of the crowd and sees a guy sprinting away across the parking lot. He is looking back to see if someone might be chasing him.

Michael immediately takes up the chase. They sprint across the huge parking lot, where the guy literally runs out of his shoes. The chase continues by jumping over a four-foot fence that borders around the park. Michael is surprised that he was able to clear it. He had never been able to do it before. They cross the street, zigzagging through the traffic, leaving the track.

Michael is slowly gaining on him. Michael chases him up the street and around a building and back onto the street, where he finally catches him. He grabs him by the collars of his shirt and pushes him up against the wall of a building and demands his money back. Now remember Michael is about 5 feet 8 inches and the other guy is well over six feet tall. Michael says, "Give me it back, you blankety, blank, blank." Suddenly, a guy stops and asks what is going on. Michael tells him that the guy stole 100 dollars from him at the track. "Did you do that?" the new guy asks. The guy Michael had been chasing answers, yes.

The new guy tells the one who stole the money to give it back to Michael. The thief takes it out of his pocket. As he goes to hand it to Michael, the other one grabs it, and pulls out a switchblade knife and points it at him. Michael backs away and the other two walk off. Michael is still adamant about getting his money back, somehow, in some way. That morning, he had been broke. Now, that hundred dollars felt as if it was a thousand to Michael. He was going to do everything possible to retrieve it. This situation was becoming very complex. Michael watched the two walk off with his $100 bill. What do I do now, he ponders. This was not the most upscale neighbourhood but Michael was still determined to somehow get his money back. He starts to trail off after them, not knowing what he will do when he has caught up to them. They get to the corner, where they both turn right. As Michael gets to the corner where they turn, a small car with four guys in it pulls up. Michael yells, "Does someone want to make 100 dollars?" One asks, "How do we do that?" Michael points to the guy walking across the lot and says, "That guy stole 100 from me. If you get it, you can have it." One of them gets out of the car and then quickly changes his mind. He gets back in and the four of them take off. Right after they left, he saw a police car coming up the street towards him. Michael gets out in the middle of the street and starts waving his arms to get him to stop. He pulls over and asks Michael, "Are you the guy who is having a problem?" Michael says, "Yes there are two fellows who stole 100 dollars from him. The one that has it just crossed that lot". Michael describes the two characters and what they wore. He tells the cop that one of them has no shoes on and is just wearing socks. He is thinking to himself, *great, the police are here to save the day.* The officer says, "Okay, you follow the one that one across the lot and I will go down the other way." He turns his car around and goes back down the way he came. Michael was so keyed up that the police were there, he didn't realize until after he was gone that he was on his own again. Michael now headed off by himself in pursuit of the guy who has his money. The two had split up and the fellow with his money headed down between a row of apartments. Michael quickly goes through the apartments and comes out to a street. When he gets to the street, he sees the street has several rows of apartments on both sides. He runs down the street, looking left and right to see if he can spot him between the rows of apartments. Michael finally spots the guy down one of the driveways between the buildings. At the end of each apartment was an 8-foot-high fence boxed at the end to keep people out. This was a local ordinance in the area to keep people out of the tenants' backyards. The guy sees him, shimmies up and over the fence and disappears. Michael quickly ran up to the point where he had seen the guy go over. Michael didn't know what to expect on the other side. Would there be more people there with the guy? As Michael came up to the fence, he looked down. Sitting there by itself was a spotted rock about the size of a baseball. Wow, how did that get there? It seemed that God was smiling down on his leprechaun. He scooped it up and jumped up. He was barely able to clamber up on the top of the fence. To his surprise, there was another fence about fifty feet away with no easy way out. The thief was about fifteen feet away, down in the enclosed area. Trapped, he was looking around furtively, not knowing where to go or what to do. Michael now felt he had the upper hand. He stood on the fence, raised his arm with the rock in his hand and yelled. "If you don't hand over my blankety, blank money right now, I am going to take this rock and crush your blankety, blankety, blank skull." The guy picked up on Michael's certain tone, born from years of throwing baseballs. He says to Michael, "Mister, mister, please don't throw the rock." He walks over to below him, pulls out the bill and hands it up to him. Michael takes the bill, then jumps down off the fence. He heads back towards the parking lot, his winnings intact. As he comes out to the street, another cop is coming along. He flags him down. He says to Michael, "Are you the guy having a problem"? Michael says yes. The cop tells him to get in the car. They drive down the street and come to where there is another police car with its lights flashing. They drive over to where a guy is spread-eagled face down on a lawn, minus his shoes. It is the original guy who took the $100. Michael lets the cop know where his shoes can be retrieved back on the parking lot of the racetrack. The cop drives him back to the lot and drops him off where his vehicle is parked. The cop then goes and retrieves the culprit's shoes for him. It had been one adventurous day, but the luck of the leprechaun had been with him. God had his angels watching over him. He had made another pot of gold. He drives home, goes into the apartment where he places the pile of cash on the table and retires to the back bedroom. When his wife finally sees the money, she squeals and yells to Michael, "Where did all this money come from?" Michael then tells of the wonderful day he had at the races. To say she was pleasantly surprised would be stating it mildly. That night they went out to a really nice restaurant and celebrated. They didn't have to eat bread and potatoes that night.

Keep reading; this all comes together as we progress. Horse racing was starting to flow in Michael's blood. That would become very much part of the leprechaun's life in the future. Michael did not pay much attention to horses for some years as he had so many varied and interesting things to keep his attention occupied. In his early thirties, Michael was a very successful entrepreneur, working long hours and making pots of gold. We talked about this when we were discussing Michael, the entrepreneur.

In 1983, on Margie's urgings, he went for a checkup with a doctor. Michael was working 20-hour days, seven days a week, with his new business and the store. He had been doing this for about four years. The doctor told him that he very much needed to do something about his way of life or he was going to end up in the hospital or worse. The doctor told him his body indicators were that of a much older person than the age he actually was. Michael was a relatively young man with a wife and two young boys, so he decided to take the doctor's advice. He gave up on a very lucrative business. He made the decision to leave California and move to southern Arizona. He purchased a new home that was being built in the suburbs of Tucson.

You may be wondering what this has to do with horses. Keep reading on and you will see how this all relates. Michael was given a date of when his new house would be ready to move into. When the time came, they sold their house in California and packed up everything for the move to Tucson. He arrives at the agreed-upon date, ready to move in, only to find the builder telling him that it is going to be another month. To say Michael was not pleased would be an understatement.

Michael asks him what he is supposed to do for another month. He had a rental truck that he did not want to be renting for another month. He asked the builder if he could store his stuff in the garage. The builder was not being helpful, so Michael decided that was it. He demanded his down payment back. He would go elsewhere. Here, he was in a new city with a wife and two children and no home. Michael, being the leprechaun he is, went into action. He started looking around for a new house to buy in the Tucson area.

Through his enquiries he somehow finds out that an old mining town called Silver Bell, now closed , has company homes for purchase for five thousand dollars each for a two-bedroom and six thousand for a three-bedroom. One then had to pay to have it moved to the location of your choice. Michael goes and looks at the houses. He decides that it is a worthwhile proposition. He purchases one with three bedrooms. In the end he buys six of them.

It is an interesting note he obtained one for his brother, one for his parents and two for other families in need. Now, he was in need of a property to put it on. He starts investigating to find land that he can purchase in the vicinity of Tucson. He quickly finds some acreage on the outskirts with access to power and water. It is a good price, so he grabs it up. In short order, he has his house moved to the new location.

In a matter of a couple of weeks, it is all set up and they move into their new residence. Michael would operate from this base very successfully for many years to come. Horses were still not part of the picture yet, but he now had enough property to support them. If this all had not happened the way it did, there is a very good possibility that the horse whisperer may never have come into being.

His life would have probably turned out very differently. It was at a horseshow sometime later where the journey began in earnest. Michael was selling cowboy hats and pins at a horse show. Next to him was another vendor selling saddles and horse tack, mainly for the western venue. Michel had his wife and two young sons with him, Michael and Patrick, who were both now teenagers. They both spent a good deal of their time at the saddle and tack booth asking that vendor many, many questions about horses.

The vendor was very patient and was happy for the company and answered all their questions. It would turn out to be very beneficial for him at the end of the show for having taken the time with them. The young boys became more and more interested in horses. They soon started badgering Michael and Margie about getting their own horses. They had been there for about a week and a half. Michel started warming up to the idea. By the end of the show, he was worn down by his boys. He talks it over with Margie. They decide to get a couple of horses. Now, we are getting somewhere. At the end of the show, they bought two saddles and all the necessary tack to go along with them. Well, they have the house to live in, and the large property for the horses but no shelter for the horses. Well, here goes the leprechaun once again.

With the help of his two sons, they built a huge wooden coral with two large exit and entry gates on either side. In the center of the coral, they erected a large sun shelter to provide shade for the horses from the intense heat of the Arizona sun. Now to find some horses. Before long, they have obtained two but then decide to get two more to make it a family deal. This means all the gear to go with them as well. Michael and his family were now the proud owners of four beautiful horses. The family was hooked. Michael and Margie now decide to build a horse barn.

Using his skills and knowledge learned in the building trades, Michael, his young sons and his father, who had moved in next door, go to work putting one together. Michael doesn't just throw together any old structure. He builds a beautiful brick-and-mortar barn that he had designed himself. It would garner much admiration and praise from all who had the opportunity to view and visit it. Michael, even though he might not have been fully consciously aware, was building for their future expansion. His skills in carpentry and building really came into play here. He would build a much larger second barn of the same quality with a vet room and hay room as his number of horses continued to expand. As you can see from the pictures on the next page, our leprechaun did things in a very professional way. When other horse owners, trainers and breeders would see his layout and workmanship, they knew that this indeed was an upscale operation and Michael had the horses to back it up.

It is interesting to note that during that time, Michael started a whole new enterprise that really was not part of the horse industry. He financed and created a backhoe excavating business called S O S Excavating. This business started with a trip to the Pima County Fair. Michael and his family took out a neighbouring couple for a day out at the fair. While at the fair, the husband wanted to go look at the new construction equipment on display. He was telling Michael that he was an excellent backhoe operator and if he had the money, he would buy one and could make a good living. Michael told him if he would run it, he would buy one and a truck and trailer to go along with it. The fellow neighbour would operate it, Michael would finance it and they would split the profits.

The neighbour was elated and agreed, so a new business partnership was formed. The new business was going very well. Unfortunately, the fellow's wife did not like him being away so much, so he stopped doing jobs and was pulling in no money. Michael had the equipment brought home. Michael then found another person to run the equipment. Some further months down the road, Michael heard that his new partner was doing jobs on his own. He was withholding it from Michael. Michael met with him and confronted him about it. Michael, again, took the equipment back. This time he sold it off and that was the end of that business. Some people, it seems, just don't recognize when they have it good. Just don't go behind the leprechaun's back. You can make many honest mistakes when dealing with a leprechaun but do not try to take advantage of him or try to steal his gold. For a awhile, this enterprise was doing well, producing gold but it was one of only a couple of endeavours that did not keep making a pot of gold because of the labour problem. In the pictures here, we see a layout from above of Michael's property and a partial view of the two beautiful brick-and-mortar horse barns he built.

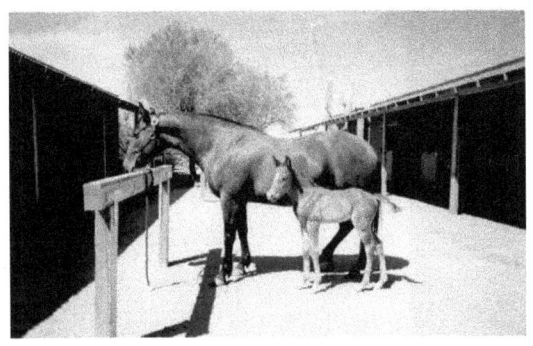

Now, let's get back to Michael and the enterprise of breeding, raising and training quarter horses. At one period in the horse business, he and his family were the proud owners of over forty horses. Michael watched and learned from what many other horse trainers and breeders did. He then applied what was successful with his own efforts. This way, he could improve upon and make better of what he observed and learned. He watched and listened to many horse trainers. From that, he was able to develop his own philosophy of how to get the best out of the horses that were in his care. He observed that there were mainly two types of training. One was the cowboy way, which was majorly forceful and dominating. Two, the no resistance way in which you worked with the horse with no force. Here is a little story of what he observed on one occasion, which emphasizes his philosophy. There was this well-known cowboy horse trainer and farrier. He was visiting and asked Michael if he could shoe one of his horses. Michael felt it would be okay so he could check out his technique. It didn't take long to find out this fellow definitely was one of those cowboys who would try to control the horse through brute force. Now Michael had his horse called Butterscotch since he was a colt. The horse was now two years old. He, of course, had been working his horse his own way and the horse was smart and very well-behaved. The farrier kept complaining that the horse was not behaving while he was working shoeing the hoof. Michael was sitting and watching what was going on. He could see the horse was not acting up at all. He tells Michael he is going to take the horse in the round pen to get him more under control.

Michael didn't want the guy to do this, but he really wanted to see how this guy operated around horses. Michael tells him okay, as he wants to see how this guy handles his horse. The guy keeps throwing his lariat at the horse and making him go faster and faster around the inside of the round pen. Michael was thinking to himself, you shouldn't be doing that, but said nothing. He wanted to see how the horse would respond to this guy's abuse. Remember here, Michael the leprechaun is a real horse whisper, and he had a very smart and well- trained horse. What do you think might happen when a horse gets treated in a negative fashion when not used to it? He kept it up, and Michael finally said out loud, you shouldn't be doing that. The fellow didn't listen and kept on doing it. Finally, the horse had enough and came to an abrupt stop. The horse knew he was being abused and was upset with this. This really, really irritated the trainer big time. He started yelling at the horse and started walking towards him. The horse turned and now stood directly facing the cowboy. Michael again yelled out you shouldn't be doing that. The cowboy didn't listen and took a step towards the horse. In an instant, the horse was in full motion, charging straight at the trainer. The guy is standing there, his mouth agape as the horse bears down on him. The horse's mouth was wide open. Before he could move, the horse rammed him and chomped down on his shoulder. The horse drove him down to the ground and then stood there looking at him. It was like he was saying, what do you think of that buddy? Thank God he did not sustain a major injury. It would be a lesson he would never forget. It had been a living lesson of what can happen with too much force being used.

Michael found out sometime later that this particular person had quite a mean streak in him when he was dealing with horses. He was working full-time at a large Arabian horse ranch as a farrier and training horses. People who boarded their horses were seeing changes occur in their horses and didn't know why. One of the other people working at the ranch observed this fellow taking horses away from the barn out behind a grove of trees. He followed him to see what was going on. He observed this trainer abusing the horse and causing the horse to become fearful and nervous. The ranch manager decided to set him up and caught him on film in the act. The fellow was field.

Michael was not surprised. Michael was glad the fellow was found out. With that kind of attitude around horses, he would do more harm than good for the horse industry.

This picture is of Michael and the first horse he bought as a young colt. He raised and trained him to be a valuable asset. He became a much desired stud horse for breeding. This is Butterscotch. In this picture, he was the Arizona Champion weaning colt. This is the same horse we talked about that a year and a half later charged the abusive farrier and trainer and taught him a lesson he wouldn't forget.

Butterscotch was guaranteed to produce a Buckskin or Palomino horse every time, no matter the colour of the mare. This horse had some very strong genes indeed. This was a very special horse for Michael, which one day almost cost Michael his life.

He had him since he was three months old. He bought him from a cowboy whom Michael knew well, who lived close by. Michael taught his horse the Horse Whisperer way. The horse was very smart and well-behaved if he was treated with love and respect. Whenever the fellow he bought the horse from was around, Butterscotch was nowhere to be seen. Michael didn't know why this was because he never did this when anyone else was around. It was quite some time later he found out through casual conversation with the guy's wife that her husband had hobbled the young horse when he was about two and a half months old as a colt. The horse never forgot. He wanted nothing to do with his original owner. The horse was, in fact, very fearful of him. Michael now understood the horse's actions whenever this cowboy was in the horse's sight.

Now, the no-resistance way would get the horse to understand and work with the trainer. Through a series of cues, such as hand signals along with simple body motions in incoordination with each other, you would get much better and lasting results when you do so. Michael would always put the horse in a classroom environment. This was to be able to teach and have the horse learn something new. It was important for the horse to know he or she was in a classroom situation, not just the trainer. Michael would only ever have two close calls when dealing with horses. Not being fully in the moment, they both nearly cost him his life. Michael's first horse was named Raz, and the owner had told him this horse was almost impossible to get into a trailer. He would somehow get the horse to Michael's place, but Michael would have to figure out how to get him back in a trailer after that. Several months down the road, Michael buys a new, four-horse, slant horse trailer. This was just a couple of weeks before Christmas.

Michael had the trailer out in the corral with Raz. He had been feeding the horse from the back of the trailer, trying to coax him to go into it. The trick of putting the feed on the back of the trailer didn't work. The horse was still terrified to go into the trailer. This is Michael's first horse, long before he became the horse whisperer he is today. On Christmas morning, Michael told Margie he was going to go out and try to teach Raz to go into the trailer. Michael has never done this, but somehow, he is going to attempt to teach him. He had his trailer inside the pen along with the horse. He tied a long rope to the front inside of the trailer, and the other end snapped onto the horse's halter, giving the horse about three feet of slack from the back of the trailer. He then took a five- foot broom handle to tap on the horse's butt to try to get him to go forward toward the trailer opening. The horse would immediately kick back with both hind legs. The horse then would swing his hind end to the other side of the trailer and Michael would have to walk around to his other side. The horse would repeat his kicking action and swing back to the other side. This dance continued for several minutes. Michael was on the right side and the horse swung back left. As Michael was walking back around to the left, he realized that there was not much space between the back of the horse, himself and the fence. At that moment, he realized if the horse kicked, he could be in trouble. As he started to turn away, the horse immediately fired both hind legs. Michael caught a hoof on his left shoulder and one to the side of his face. He was thrown about fifteen feet back. As he lay on the ground in agonizing pain, all he could say was Jesus, Jesus, Jesus. Thank God his son Patrick was there Watching. He ran as fast as he could to the house to tell his mother. A broken shoulder and a very swollen face resulted in a long and very painful recuperation. Michael had to have five pins put in the shoulder to repair it. The pins are still in there to this very day. The Doctor told him it was the worst shoulder he had ever worked on. It was a lesson he would not likely ever forget.

It was a situation he would not find himself in again. Michael was pretty much laid up until his body was somewhat healed up. He decided he had better learn how to be able to get a horse into a trailer with ease and with the horse's cooperation this next time around.

The next time, his leprechaun luck might run out. One of the reasons for Michael's success has been his willingness and ability to observe what others did with their horses. What worked, he would work on to improve it; what didn't would be thrown out. Like everything Michael does, it is done with the idea to learn and to do it right. With this in mind, Michael was told by a fellow horse owner how he could guarantee to get any horse to go into a trailer. He observed this taking place and was able to duplicate it to where he could get any horse into a trailer safely. Sometime later, he heard about a seminar another horse trainer was giving on getting horses into trailers. Michael was sceptical but decided he was going to go check it out. Michael figured he would be there to help the guy out if he failed to get the horse in the trailer. This trainer again said he could guarantee one hundred percent that one could learn to easily get a horse into a trailer. Michael watched and came away from that seminar pleasantly surprised, knowing it was an improvement upon what he knew. He could improve upon it to ensure he could train any horse to go into a trailer with no effort. He could train a horse who had never been in a trailer or a horse who had been in trailers but was very fearful of entering one. By teaching certain cues, he could change the horse's attitude and thinking. The horse could then be easily loaded into the trailer with no hesitation or fear. Michael put in the time it took and would not stop until the horse would walk into the trailer easily and calmly, of its own accord. Working with the horse's willingness and lots of patience, you have a calm, trained horse where no excess force is needed. Again, Michael would put in the time it took, depending on the situation. Using the horse whisperer way was well worth the time. In the end, one would have a calm and well-trained horse. Michael had this one young horse he had taught this procedure. The horse just loved going into the trailer, so much so that he made a game of it. It would, in fact, gallop from thirty or more yards away into the trailer with such exuberance it would skid to a stop on impacting the front of the trailer stall. By the way, this trailer was out in the open. This horse could go anywhere he wanted but would always go into the trailer. Michael really liked this horse as it mirrored in many ways how this leprechaun viewed his life as a game he enjoyed. When people would come over to visit, Michael would get this horse to do his thing. The people viewing this would be in awe. It was an experience they would enjoy remembering. Michael had neighbours, a husband and wife, next door to his place. They were heavily involved in the rodeo circuit. They had this one horse who had been terrified for years of going into a trailer. It had put many, many visible dents in the back of the trailer as high as the top of the door to prove it. The door had to be welded on several times because the horse had kicked it off its hinges. This horse was fortunate he did not break a leg at some point. This one morning, they are once again trying to force this horse into a trailer. Michael was outside, tending to his horses. Michael can see and hear the ruckus from his neighbour's yard as they are attempting to get the horse in the trailer. It is the day before they will be participating in a rodeo. He thinks to himself, if they keep that up, someone is going to get seriously hurt. Michael knows perfectly well what can happen as he has had his own painful experience. When he goes back into the house, he tells Margie, that somebody is going to get hurt out there. It is lunchtime, and his wife has just made him a couple of BLTs and homemade French fries. He is going to sit down to watch a football game on the TV. There is a knock on his door; it is his neighbour, Brian. He tells Michael his wife has been injured by the horse. He is wondering if Michael might be able to come and help get Rags in the trailer. Brian knows Michael is good at getting horses into trailers. Brian says, "You just come and lead him up to the trailer. I will beat his butt until he goes in the trailer."

Michael says, "So you want me to come over and have happen to me what happened to Kim." If that is what you want, you can leave. I will sit here, eat my sandwich and watch the game." The fellow realizes he has overstepped and sheepishly says okay, then, more politely, asks, 'Will you please come and help." Michael tells him on one condition only. You and Kim can sit in the yard and watch. If I hear one word out of any of either one of you, I am going home. Brian, of course, agrees, and Michael gets ready to go. When they get there, Michael takes the halter and lead rope and walks the horse down an easement road out of sight. He takes the horse away out of sight of the trailer as he doesn't want the horse to be upset by seeing the trailer. Michael will be gaining his trust and will be teaching him some cues. Michael explains the main cue was to teach this horse to move forward calmly every time he was asked to do so. Once he was willing to move forward each and every time he asked him, he would eventually get him to go into the trailer all on his own. The force method Kim and Brian used caused someone to get hurt. Michael was using his four-step method, as was stated at the beginning of this chapter. I don't get hurt, the horse does not get hurt, the horse learns a new lesson, and the horse remains calm. The four-step method went into effect the moment he took the horse away. After Michael had built the necessary foundation of cooperation with Rags, he brought it back into view of the trailer. He then works back and forth to the trailer's mouth from about a hundred feet. With a lot of coaxing and validating, Rags, has just been taught to obey and follow the cues. He was able to get Rags to eventually put one front foot in the trailer, then two, then one back foot, then finally all four. He would immediately take Rags back out and repeat the process again, many more times. Finally, when he feels Rags is ready, he walks back about thirty feet and gives the horse the cue to go forward. He does this several times. Michael then takes him back once more to the thirty-foot mark. Again, he goes forward towards the trailer. This time, Michael stops at the 15-foot mark that he had previously put there. He lets go of the lead rope. Rags keeps on going. Rags could go anywhere but casually walk up to the entrance and calmly step into the trailer without hesitation. This is a condensed version of his actual training routine. This training is done correctly, as Michael did; the results that are intended to happen always do so. The couple had been sitting back in the yard watching. The husband had to go into the house to answer the phone, so he didn't see the horse go into the trailer on his own. When he came back out, his wife was yelling very loudly and excitedly. Did you see that Rags just went into the trailer all by himself? Michael took the horse out of the trailer and repeated so they both could see. To say they were amazed and delighted is no small understatement. As a side note, after every rodeo they did had ended, many people would come to see the circus of Brian, trying to get Rags back in the trailer. Needless to say, there were a bunch of open mouths when, this time, they observed a completely opposite scenario of what usually took place. This had taken a good part of the afternoon, but at the end of the class, this horse would casually go into the trailer with no resistance and be very, very calm. Of course, all were amazed, but not Michael. He was a Horse Whisperer and a leprechaun to boot. He knew his stuff. Michael missed his football game but had probably saved someone from a major injury or even their life by what he had done for them with Rags.

Another Grand Slam for this game-playing leprechaun. Being in the horse business, one always needs to show the horse so it can be compared to other horses in the same category. The more and better you show, the more you win. He quickly became very good at it and was soon winning many ribbons and buckles. Michael loved the sport of horse racing, and it didn't take him very long to become involved in the racing scene. Michael acquired some great runners and put many winning races behind him. Before I met Michael and got the scoop from him about the quarter horse racing industry, I had no idea how it was run. I learned that it sometimes had a dark, nasty underbelly. The big boys in the game did not play fair at all. It was so bad that Michael feared for the life of one of his best horses. Michael had this beautiful young stallion who was definitely the fastest horse in the region he competed in. The region semi-finals were being held up in Wyoming. He and Margie loaded up their horse and headed north to race their horse. There were three qualifying races. The top horse of each heat would then be in the final race to determine who would race for the top prize in southern Cal in the fall. Michael easily won his heat with no question. Now, this is where the corruption raised its ugly head. Michael's horse and rider were called out for an error, which did not happen. It was a lie. His horse was put in fourth place and penalized with time taken off. Even with all this BS, the horse still had the fastest time, so it would be in the finals. After the race, he was visited by the head vet. She said she had heard the horse may have been injured in the race. The fact was, the horse had a bruised foot, so Michael wanted to have the farrier put on special aluminium shoes to dampen the extra pressure in the next race. The track was brutally hard where the races were taking place. The vet asked Michael a statement-like question, "You are not going to race him in the final, are you?" Michael told her he didn't know and would decide as they got nearer to race day, which was two weeks away. Now, to better see the intrigue, it should be noted that the Vet was the wife of the trainer who called on Michaels Horse.

The trainers' horse ended up being third in the heat. It was shortly after this that the father of the rider ended up first. Came to see Michael. He told Michael that he had heard rumours around the track that Michael's horse was in danger and he should take his horse home. Something very bad could befall it. Needless to say, Michael and Margie were very upset. The leprechaun, however, was no quitter. He moved their horse out of the main barn to another barn, well away from the other horses. They put the horse in a stall at the farthest end of the barn, away from any doors. They then backed their truck up against the stall door so no one could get near the horse other than going through the back of the truck. He and his wife, between the two of them stayed with the horse 24/7 for two weeks straight until the final race. No one could get near the horse to cause any harm to it. This same unfortunate unethical practice that was used to disqualify him caused Michael to lose many races where he really had won. As I stated earlier, the good old boy network has a dark side to it. Michael did run his horse in the final and won handily. He would be racing in the Champion of Champions show on ESPN National TV race in at Los Alamitos in southern California in November.

The picture is of Michael's horse, who won.

He was the fastest quarter horse in the United States. Unfortunately, the horse ended up having three cracks occur in the right front shin as the ground they were racing on was very dry and hard. The shenanigans continued back in California. Michael was working on his horse on a regular basis to get him healed and ready to run the Champion of Champions race in Los Alamitos in November. His regular trainer was very busy in Arizona. He couldn't be training his horse in California as well. Michael calls the head of the AQHA racing division and is told he can get him a trainer at that track. This track is world famous for having the fastest horses in the world train and race there. Michael drives to the racetrack to take his horse to the new trainer, whom he has not met yet. He pulls up to the guard gate on the back side of the track. That's where the horses are stabled. Security calls for the trainer to come down and meet Michael at the gate. While he is waiting, a young jockey, who Michael knows well, walks over and starts talking to Michael. His name is Joe Padilla. He is one of the top jockeys at the track. He tells Michael the whole track is buzzing about what he has in his trailer as they are talking about two people walking towards them at the gate. It is his new trainer, along with the number one jockey at the track, G R Carter. He has been number one for several years running.

The trainer introduces himself and the Jockey and tells Michael this jockey will be riding his horse in the big race. Three weeks before the big race, the new trainer calls up Michael. He says there is a race coming up and would like to race his horse so he would have the experience of running at night. Michael was not in agreement. The plan was just to run the horse in the big race. He and Margie had set their sights on just running the Champion of Champions race. The trainer finally convinces Michael to go for it. It was with many reservations and against what the leprechaun thought best for their horse. It would turn out to be a big mistake for all concerned. His horse ran a great race and came in a very close second. Unfortunately, the horse reinjured the leg that had been injured at the big race in Wyoming. Every day for the next two weeks before the big race, Michael had the top vet come to check on the horse day by day and let him know how well the horse was doing. He told Michael he would let him know by the big race day if he felt the horse was well enough to run. Now, the jockey who was scheduled to be the rider decided not to ride him in this race. He knew the horse was not a hundred percent. When Joe, the other top jockey, hears about this, he comes to see Michael. He tells him, if you are going to race him, I will ride him for you. Michael lets him know that he may not race him, and if he does, he won't be running at full capacity. Joe tells him again, that is okay; if you run him, I will ride him. When the race day was on them, the vet told Michael that the horse could race but would be running about seventy-five percent of his capacity. Michael asked him what he felt his chances were that he might break down in this race. He told Michael that the horse had a one in ten chance of breaking down. Michael told him, please do not tell me it is a one in ten if it is; in fact, it is one in five.

The vet assured Michael it was one in ten. On the evening of the race, Michael goes to his car to get dressed for the race. He does some heartfelt praying to God to please see that his horse does not break down in this race. He would be happy with last place as long the horse doesn't break down. Michael's horse runs the big race. It was very painful for the horse, but even so, he ended up coming in a very close second. The jockey told him it had been a very scary ride. He told Michael every time the horse's injured leg hit the ground, the horse shuddered. All in all, it was quite a frustrating experience indeed for Michael and Margie. He didn't win and get the gold only because of the injury to the horse. Without that injury, he surely would have gotten the full pot of gold. Below is a picture of the trophy he and the other ten finalists received.

Here is another story that illustrates how blatant corruption can be within the horse racing industry. Michael was doing the fair racing circuit in Arizona and was racing his horse, Miss Villa Hempen. A young female jockey, Anna Bario, came to talk to Michael a couple of days before Michael's horse would race. She told him she really wanted to be the jockey on his horse on the next race day. Anna had raced the day before, and she had been injured and was bruised and wearing some bandages. Michael had told her no, she needed to recuperate, and she could ride his horse in another race. She implored him to let her ride his horse. She told Michael she had ridden other horses in races against his horse, but all she ever saw was his horse's butt. She started doing jumping jacks to show she was okay to Ride. Michael gave in, and if his trainer said okay, she could ride. The trainer said it is your horse, Michael, so you can have whoever you want to ride. Anna rides his horse to a first-place finish. Michael's horse is then disqualified.

Michael was walking by the announcer later that day. He mentioned to the announcer he couldn't figure out why his horse was taken down. His horse and jockey had not done anything wrong. The announcer said, I know Michael. He tells Michael he had been at the restaurant early in the Morning. The stewards were there as well. He overheard them talking. They were discussing Anna. They blamed Anna for the problem that had occurred in the race she was hurt in the day before. He heard them say that the next race Anna ran, if and when she won, they were going disqualify her horse to take her down. The next race was, of course, Michael's horse. Because Anna was the winner, the horse was taken down. He was next racing her at the Flagstaff Fairgrounds Racetrack In northern Arizona two weeks later. He had to use a different jockey this time as Ann was still under suspension from Prescott.

At this race, the horse fell to its knees out of the starting gate. The rider stayed on, and the horse was able to get up. It quickly started chasing the rest of the horses down the track. Despite the earlier stumble, she circles the field. The jockey was able to bring in the horse to a clear second place. The race was no sooner finished when an enquiry was up on the board on his horse. The horse and rider were said to have done something wrong. The horse's second-place finish was disqualified and placed him last. The boos from the grandstand were a roar when the fans saw what had been unfairly done. The next day, the jockey was called in before the stewards of the racing board.

Michael didn't have to go but decided to go see why his horse was taken out of the second-place finish. The jockey went in first. Normally, when a jockey is called in for the horse that he rode, he gets a suspension and a fine. When he comes out, he tells Michael that they didn't do anything to him. That meant they were going after Michael and his horse. Michael goes in and sits before the stewards. They watch the film of the race. Michael observes that the horse and jockey do nothing wrong during the race, and indeed, they win a clean, commanding second place. During the replay of the race, the stewards keep saying, do you see that? Do you see that? Michael's horse is nowhere near any other horse. He keeps saying see what. Of course, nothing further occurred. Some years later, at Turf Paradise in Arizona, a friend of Michaels, who was a jockey, told him he was being looked at by the racing board to become a steward himself. He was told by the other members that the board was the prosecutor, the Judge, and the Jury in all cases. There was no possible way of disputing their decisions. The jockey, shortly after that meeting, became one. The next season, he was racing one of his horses in Globe, Arizona. She was another fast horse.

Michael and Margie took some friends with them to watch the races. Michael's jockey was not available, so the trainer had to pick one he didn't know. Michael and Margie's horse is figured to be one of the top horses in the race that day. Michael's horse jumped out in the lead from the gate, and she should have been a winner. Michael watched from behind the gate and observed the jockey never used the stick on her butt one time. This is unusual, as in quarter horse racing, as the jockey always uses the stick. Michael's horse was not even in the money.

Michael went back to the barn to check on his horse. On his way back to the grandstands, he sees a horse trainer leaning against a fence. Michael asks him how it is going. The guy says, wonderful, he has winning tickets for the first four races and is going to win in all the next races. Michael told him that it was BS. If my horse would have run the way she could, you wouldn't have cashed a ticket in the fourth. The trainer tells him there is a jockey who tells him all the first-place winners for all the races. That most definitely opened up the leprechaun's eyes. He asks the fellow who is going to win the next race. The fellow tells him, so Michael decides to place a bet and make a few bucks back to feel better about the loss from the race he should have won. After the races are over, they head back to the barns where the vehicle is parked. He sees the trainer walk up to a pickup in the parking lot. He reaches into his pocket, pulls out a wad, and reaches into the passenger side of the vehicle through the window. He drops the wad inside.

This was the big payoff for all the winning tips given. Of all things, the leprechaun was there to see it. Michael's thoughts on this are that maybe the jockeys get together every so often and work out who is going to be the winner in certain races. They do this to make a little extra income to supplement what they need. The regular payouts for most of them do not pay a lot on a regular basis. It all goes down to show what can happen around the stewards or the jockeys.

A couple of months later, back home, Michael is preparing for foaling and breeding seasons for his mares and outside mares that he looks after. Michael set up a special stall in the barn to be a birthing stall, which also has an outside pen. It had cameras in and out, where he could monitor what was going on. Here, Michael learned all the ins and outs of the birthing procedure. Through the years, he aided with over 30 of them. He became so good he could predict the day when a mare was going to give birth. He told me a story of a lady who lived down the road from him who was a new horse owner. One morning, she came out to see her horse and found a dead foal lying outside the fence. She hadn't even been aware her mare was in foal. She called Michael and told him what had happened and asked him if he would please come.

He goes over to see her. He could see she was obviously very upset. Trying to console her, Michael asks her, would you like to have a new baby horse next year? He tells her that if she would like that to happen, he will breed her mare with his stallion. She will have a beautiful new baby horse. She tearfully tells him, thank you, yes, that would be wonderful. Now, Michael normally charged a five-hundred-dollar stud fee for his horse, which was very reasonable. He would do this to help her mentally get over her loss. He told her when her mare is getting ready to deliver her Foal next season, he will be there to help ensure it all comes off well. He would come every day to check on the horse near the end. The lady was almost in a panic mode, worrying it would be déjà vu. Michael told her not to go out and check every day and get herself all worked up. He told her I will tell you the night she is going to birth her foal, and that is the only time to worry, but I will be there to make sure it all works out okay. He would tell her when it was going to be born.

When the day finally comes, Michael goes to sleep in his easy chair with his clothes on. He told her to check on the mare that night and to call me when she saw these signs. She calls Michael at about midnight. Michael is there within minutes to help the mare and the birthing of her foal. It all goes well with no complications. The mare presents the world with a new beautiful golden palomino, appaloosa foal. Michael tells her she is going to get many offers for that colt but take nothing less than 5,000 if she decides to sell it. She tells him she has no intention of selling it. She profusely thanks Michael for all his help and caring. The leprechaun has done it again.

Michael told me of a story where he again could have lost his life. He was taking his stallion, Butterscotch, whom he had bred with many, many mares, out to breed once again. Every mare he had bred prior was bred at that same spot. The mare was out behind a tree and tied to a breeding pole. The stallion, although he could not see her, knew she was there and was, of course, very eager to perform his duty. Michael was walking the horse up on the left side with a lead rope. As they came up to the tree, the horse was very excited and tried to cut the corner around the tree. Michael was going to be jammed in against the tree. Michael had to give the horse a little more lead, then pulled back slightly on the rope. He was a little too close to his horse. The stallion kicked back forcefully. He fired both hind legs and caught Michael fully in the chest.

The horse did not intentionally kick Michael; he was just in a hurry to get to the mare. Michael went flying back and ended up with several broken ribs and couldn't catch his breath. The stallion was so into doing his stud work that he just momentarily forgot everything else. A very slight change in normal procedure and a very freaky incident had nearly cost him his life. The leprechaun would survive. He would make sure that situation would never happen again.

Whenever Michael was having his horses shod, he would always watch and ask questions. After some time, he asked his farrier if he would show him how to do it. The farrier, who was very well known, told him many people asked him, but he was reluctant, as most wouldn't follow through. It was also dangerous; many farriers received serious injuries from the hoof of a horse, either from being kicked or from getting trampled. At least two farriers each year in the US lose their lives while doing farrier work.

Michael told him, "I am not your average horse owner. When I say I want to learn, I mean it! "The farrier had known Michael for some time by then. He could see Michael was telling the truth, so he agreed to teach him. Michael, in due course, became very proficient at it. Interestingly enough, his two sons, Michael and Patrick, wanted to follow in Dad's footsteps. Both went to Farrier School to become certified professionals.

Michael trained in Arizona, and Patrick trained in Denver, Colorado. I talked to Patrick, his one son, and asked him how he had liked it. He told me it was a very satisfying profession but was very hard on the body's knees and back. Both he and his brother gave it up to find something that wasn't so hard on their bodies. Even though they enjoyed the work, Patrick also told me the main reason he gave it up was the constant interference from the clients he was servicing. Many of them thought they knew better than the farrier. One of his clients kept badgering him as he was working on her horse. Patrick finally had enough of her interference. He took off his tool belt and chaps and then handed them to her. He told her, here, take these and show me how it is done. She said no more to Patrick. I found out that the profession held a yearly show where they would compete against others in the industry. Both of Michael's sons loved the competition and did very well. As a farrier, there is much more education and skill needed than just to shoe horses. It is almost the same as a foot doctor fitting out someone for special orthopaedic shoes and inserts. So, when Michael was looking after forty-plus horses, he rarely needed the services of an outside farrier with three of them in the household.

Now let's get back to Michael and his abilities as a Horse Whisperer. When Michael told me that there was probably no one else like him in the whole world, I tended to believe him. He has shared with me things about horses and his abilities that I would probably not hear anywhere else. I really think that this is where the leprechaun and his talents show up.

Michael has the ability to train a horse with really no effort or force and get the horse's willingness to do anything he asks of it. If you look at this next picture, you can see Michael with a horse he was teaching not to spook or be easily startled. He could get to the point of completely covering the horse's head so it couldn't see and then snap a buggy whip near its face. It would snap so loud it sounded like a gun had gone off. The horse would just stand there calmly as if nothing at all was happening. The whole purpose is to not have a fearful horse but to have a calm one. This, again, is the skill of a Horse Whisperer.

The secret is to get the horse to trust you, for it to know you have its best interest at heart. Through these actions, the horse will become spook-proof. The horse knows that you mean it no harm.

Here is another interesting story to show Michael's skill as a horse whisperer:

Michael's two sons were working as professional farriers at a large dude ranch in southern Arizona. In all, they were looking after 80-plus horses. There was one horse there called Rosie. She was a beautiful, dappled grey horse but had acquired some bad habits. She had caused serious injury to three of the riders who worked at the ranch. The ranch owner was beside herself with this horse. She was looking to possibly put Rosie down if the horse couldn't be turned around in a short period of time. When Michael and Patrick heard this, they approached her with a better solution. When Patrick and his brother first started working for the ranch owner, she had told Patrick that her personal and favourite horse she liked to ride had been lame for some time. She had other farriers look at her horse, but no one had been able to fix the problem. She asked Patrick if he could take a look to see if he might be able to figure it out.

He took a quick look and told her yes, he could right the horse. Patrick worked on the horse, and in a couple of days, the horse was completely sound. The owner was very grateful. She had asked Patrick if he knew anyone who could help sort out the horse Rosie. Patrick told her to give his Dad a call. If there was one person who could fix up Rosie, it was him. She was more than happy to give Michael a call. She immediately called Michael and told him what was happening with her horse, Rosie.

Above is a picture of Michael, his brother Don, and his two farrier sons, Michael and Patrick.

Michael told her he could turn her horse around but needed to take the horse to his ranch. He told her it would take approximately 30 to 45 days working with her horse to get Rosie retrained and fully under control. She readily agreed. Michael picked up the horse a couple of days later and took her to his ranch. He worked with her daily using the techniques he had developed until the horse was fully under control and a changed horse. Before the agreed time, he returned Rosie back to her ranch. Michael would demonstrate to her that she could be confident in and be proud to have her back at the ranch and ready to go to work.

This ranch catered to a worldwide clientele. There were many people from several European countries staying here at any given time. While these guests were there, the ranch owner had invited the guests to come and watch a special training session with a horse named

Rosie. Michael put Rosie in a sixty-foot diameter training pen to show what had been accomplished with Rosie.

He told everyone, first, he was going to work with her on the ground. Before he does each demonstration step, he tells his audience exactly what he is going to do and how the horse will respond. This is so those watching can follow along and see the results each time.

Many of the guests were now standing and sitting outside the fence to watch the show. Michael spent a good hour using nothing more than the cues and signals, showing that the horse was totally willing to do anything he asked of it. He could start and stop her at will, at any point, make her stand and not move, have her trot, run, and gallop. He could walk up to her, around her, and walk away, and the horse would not move an inch unless he gave her a signal to do so. The owner and guests were very impressed.

Michael then put the horse in the middle of the pen, facing the crowd. He again explains to the owner and spectators what he is going to do next. He tells them he is going to saddle her up and ride her around the pen. He then tells them he is going to fully open the twelve-foot gate right in front of them. He is then going to go out to the hitching post, which is a good twenty feet outside the pen. He is going to retrieve the blanket, the saddle, and the halter. Each round trip is about 100 feet. Rosie is not going to move an inch while he does this. He then goes to the large entrance and exit gate on the side of the pen and opens it up completely. The saddle blanket, the saddle, and the bridle are sitting on the hitching post. He walks out of the pen over to the hitching post, picks up the blanket, and then heads back towards Rosie.

She has not moved at all. He puts the blanket on her, and again, she does not move. He turns and walks back across the pen and out the gate once again to the hitching rail. He retrieves the saddle and carries it back, puts it on the horse, then cinches it up. The horse still stands patiently. Now for the true test. Michael walks back and retrieves the bridal. He again walks back to the front of Rosie. He gives a hand signal, and Rosie lowers her head down to almost the height of Michael's waist so he can easily slip it on. Now, this is unusual because a horse will normally lift its head up when it sees the bridal. This is mainly because it really doesn't like the idea of the bit in its mouth.

What had been witnessed by those watching was a calm, well-behaved horse, much more than the usual one would see on a trained horse. This was, in fact, quite beyond the normal, especially on a horse that was out of control just thirty-plus days ago. So now the horse is saddled up and ready to ride. Rosie continues to stand in the same position. Michael tells the people watching he is now going to mount Rosie, and she will follow all his cues like she did when he was working with her on the ground.

Michel mounts into the saddle. He drops the reins on her neck and tells the owner and guests what he is going to do. This is so that they will know what is happening over the next 30 minutes as he works with Rosie. He now demonstrates her willingness to follow all his cues as she did while he was on the ground. Rosie's owner and the assembled crowd were in awe of how the two of them worked together.

After the demonstration, the ranch manager yells out. She does well in the pen, but how will she be on a ride? Michael thinks to himself, what an inane question, but answers, "She will be the same on the ride as she did here." She is a completely different horse," the ranch owner exclaims. "I am so happy you were able to do this. I sure didn't want to put her down." Shall we go for a ride and see how she behaves? Rosie's owner asks Michel. Yes, let's do that now he replies. She lets some of the ranch crew and manager who wanted to go on a ride get saddled up. They were soon out on their ride, and of course, Rosie was on her best behaviour. Can we gallop her, the owner asks. Sure, let's do it Michael responds, and they are off, leaving the rest behind in a cloud of dust. We were way ahead, so we stopped to let the others catch up. While we were waiting, she said in all my years, I have never seen or witnessed what you and Rosie did back there. She asked me how I did you do that. I told her that is what I do.

Again, she thanks Michael for saving and returning a great horse to her. She tells Michael she can't believe there has been such a big change in Rosie. When they return from the ride, Michael asks her who was going to be her rider. He would like to go over the various signals with him so she would behave the same way for him as she did for me after Michael was gone. While he was doing his demonstration with Rosie, a group of riders came in, led by, as Michael described him, a fellow who dressed like and was a spitting image of John Wayne. He could have been John Wayne's double in the movies with his drawl, hat, scarf, boots, and jacket.

He was really playing up the part. Now, back to who was going to be her rider. If you guessed John Wayne, good. The next day, Michael was there early to go over with John Wayne the cues to ride and control Rosie. When he gets there, he sees the new rider leaning on the fence, watching Rosie eating hay some fifty yards away. Michael walks up and asks are you ready to saddle her and check her out? John Wayne looks at Michael and says, sure if you can catch her. I have tried several times, and she just runs away. Michael says, "Check this out". Michael steps through the fence and yells, "Rosie." The horse immediately stops eating, turns, and looks at him. He then gives her a hand signal, and she immediately walks over to him and stops. The surprised cowboy asks, "How did you do that?" Michael tells him, "That is what I am here for today, to teach you so you will get the best from

Rosie." Michael rides Rosie around for some time, going over the cues to show John how Rosie responds. After he has finished, he asks John, "Do you want to use mine or your own saddle?" The cowboy indicates his own saddle, so Michael takes off his, and they put John's saddle on Rosie.

The cowboy mounts, and Michael asks him to take the horse to rail and walk her a few times around the inside of the pen. Michael tells him, Start trotting her. There is no change as he continues walking Rosie. Get her trotting, Michael again tells him. John still keeps walking her. Once more, Michael tells him to start her trotting. The rider still keeps the horse walking. What's the problem? Michael asks him. "I'm scared," John replies. John Wayne was still stuck in the past and remembering how Rosie used to be.

Michael knew, then, that was not the horse for him. He tells the rider to dismount and tells him this is not the horse for him. He then goes and tells the owner what has occurred. She tells Michael, I have another rider for Rosie. I will get him. The new rider catches on quickly, and the horse and rider are soon in sync. A couple of months later, Michael went back to see how the new rider and Rosie were doing. Fantastic, the rider retorts, the best horse I have ever ridden. Michael smiled to himself. The Horse Whisperer, alias, the leprechaun, had done his magic again. Another calm and well-trained horse. It is another big walk-off home run.

In 1996, Michael and his wife were running the ranch by themselves. Their two sons had left and were doing their own thing. Michael and Margie decided to sell. They moved into the house he had obtained for his brother. Don and his wife Linda had moved back to California a year before. The house was unsold and sitting empty. The two would take the house over until it was sold. During that time, Michael and Margie split up; Margie, in the meantime, started working for a man who owned a large machining plant in Tucson. He had a horse ranch with several horses that at one time had been wild, but he wanted to give them a good home so they would be safe. He didn't have time to look after them as he was working so much. He asked Michael's wife if she knew anyone who could train and look after his horses. Margie told him the best person would be my husband. Her boss quickly hired Michael to look after his ranch and train his horses. His son Patrick was also working for him at his plant at that time. Michael continued to work there for some time, looking after the horses and taking care of the ranch.

Eventually, Michael found it too upsetting to remain where he would daily be reminded of his wife. He made the decision to move well out of town. He bought a thirty-six-acre piece of property in Suni zona, about two and a half hours east of Tucson. It had originally been a forty-acre piece, but the owner had kept four acres that had a house on it. Michael's property was fully fenced. It had several nice corrals, a large arena, a round pen, and a hot walker. He then bought a travel trailer to live in. There was an old barn on the property that he made part of into living quarters that came out quite nice. Michael was getting into more racing, so he decided he would build a 3/8-mile race track to train his horses on. He went to Tucson and measured off the racetrack called Rillito Park racetrack.

He then went and marked off the place on his property to pretty much duplicate the track in Tucson. He next went and bought a couple of tractors to plough and smooth out the area where he was going to make his track. Michael's plan was to be there for the long haul.

A few months later, the owner of the four acres with the house decided to sell it. From the moment the new owner moved in, he started harassing and doing things that were definitely not friendly and had designs on Michael to sell and move. Michael suspected and did find out he was dealing in drugs and human smuggling. He would stand on his back porch and point his rifle at Michael as if he was going to shoot him.

Michael finally told him he was tired of him pointing his rifle at him. He yells back, "One of these times, I am not just going to point it at you; I am going to take care of you." Michael's two dogs died suspiciously. He later found poisoned meat inside his fence. Some of his horses started to get sick. It was becoming dangerous and out of hand.

The local sheriff, who just lived a quarter mile away, was constantly coming over and telling Michael if he didn't stop harassing his neighbour, he would run him in. The guy was accusing Michael of the things he was actually doing to Michael and more. This guy was always going out in the middle of the night down the road that went away from civilization. Michael one time tried to find out in the middle of the night where this guy was going and what he was up to. It was a real cat and mouse game, and he almost was caught, so he didn't do it again. Michael felt the deputy was somehow part of the guy's operation. This harassment went on for over a year and a half. It was reaching a tipping point. Michael concluded he had one of two options. One was to do the guy in before he did him in, or two, sell and move on with his life. After some heartfelt prayer with God, he decided on option two. He sold and moved on.

It is interesting to note that six months later, Michael found out that the guy's wife had murdered him. What goes around does seem to come around. When you fool around and mistreat a leprechaun, good things don't happen to you. In this case, the fellow paid the ultimate price with his own life. Michael now needed to find a new game to play where he could hit some home runs.

In 2002, Michael started a whole new phase in his life as a Horse Chiropractor and therapist. He soon became very successful at it and was very much in demand by owners and trainers of racehorses in Southern California. Michael was so proficient in his skill that he was the only one trusted to treat the horses of many of the trainers and owners in some of the biggest racetracks in the nation, such as Hollywood Park, Santa Anita, Del Mar, and more. He first honed his skills in Turf Paradise in Phoenix, then moved to the big tracks in California.

He went as far afield as Churchill Downs for the breeders' cup in 2010 and, in 2012, for his favourite trainer whose horse, I'll Have Another, had won the Kentucky Derby, The Preakness, and hopes to complete the Triple Crown at Belmont.

His Horse Chiropractic career all started when a farrier was working on one of his horses. He noticed that the horse seemed to be stiff. He told Michael that there might be something he could do to fix it. He starts to feel some muscles on the horse's neck and back. He then starts to message muscles in the area. Michael noticed the horse seemed to greatly relax and really enjoyed it. The fellow then explains to Michel what he has been doing. Michael was immediately interested. He started thinking this was something he might be able to do. The wheels in his mind started turning once again. He started treating some of his own horses and seeing what results could be obtained.

This was to be the beginning of another major phase in his life. Michael, as with everything he decides to do, attacks it with the idea of being the very best he can be. He will be as professional as he can with it. He started watching and treating horses. He started going to the library to read more, educate himself, and study the skeletal and muscular structures of horses so he could be more informed. He started treating his own horses on a regular basis and began seeing very positive results with what he was doing. He also treated horses in many different venues, rodeo horses, and barrel racers. Roping horses, hunter jumpers, and the list goes on. He was always able to fix the problem, and his skills became better and better.

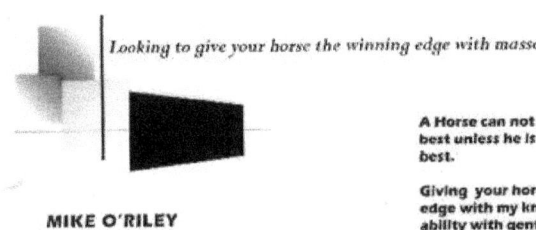

MIKE O'RILEY

520-405-4258

A Horse can not give his very best unless he is feeling his very best.

Giving your horse the winning edge with my knowledge and ability with gentle corrective care of the back and spinal muscles.

This is a card he created that he would give out to horse trainers or owners. As you can see, it shows the skeletal and muscle structure of the horse. This, Michael, knew inside and out like he knew the back of his hand. This card saved a lot of explaining. Slowly, Michael started to build a reputation amongst trainers and owners of racehorses. Michael started his work in Arizona, but He soon went back to Southern Cal, where were stabled the majority of the top thoroughbreds. He came back to Arizona occasionally when he was asked to. His production of great results on these horses continued to grow and become known in the racing circles. Unfortunately, in almost any field of endeavour, there seems to be one or more persons who feel somehow threatened by someone else's knowledge and success. They then try to squelch it. In Michael's case, it was the head veterinarian in California. She was appointed to the position by the governor. She came up to him one day and told him he could not treat horses on race day. If he did, he would lose his license.

Now, to note, there is nothing written in the horse racing rule book that says you can't treat a horse on race day. It states that the trainer of the horse that is going to race that day has an obligation to do whatever he feels is necessary, that is, legal, to ensure the horse is in the best possible condition to race.

It was one day at the track, the day of a big race, and a trainer asked Michael to look at one horse and see if he could help the horse who would be racing that day.

Michael was a little cautious and looked around to see if the head vet was anywhere close. Not seeing her, he agreed to check out the horse. He soon found the area and began to massage the muscle. As he is working his magic on the horses, Stall, the head vet, comes walking down through the barn. She sees Michael working on a horse and walks over to him. She yells at him, "What are you doing there, Mike? I told you before not to treat a horse on race day."

She tells Michael she is going to have him brought up before the racing board and have him stripped of his license for disobeying her order. A date is set for Michael to come before the racing board. A friend of

Michael, who is also a lawyer, whose horse Michael has treated successfully, hears about what this vet is doing. He agrees to represent Michael Pro bono. Michael shows up at the appointed time for his hearing. During the hearing, the strangest thing happens. The Vet starts testifying about Michael defying her order. She, then, jumps off the deep end and actually starts yelling and swearing, generally making a fool of herself. It is a rather incredulous display to watch. She could be heard outside the door in another room. The board decides in Michael's favour. He is free to continue to treat horses when needed. They also make a recommendation for him to get certified by the state as well. Michael agrees to obtain the certification. It takes two weeks to get it done. Michael is surprised at how little the certifiers know. He, in fact, ends up teaching them things they didn't know. They are, in fact, very impressed with Michael's knowledge and skill. The Vet was removed from her position, so it was no longer a problem.

Once more, it just goes to show; watch out when you try to abuse a leprechaun even if the Governor appoints you. Michael continued his practice and was so skilled at what he did that he was always in high demand on all the major racetracks on the West Coast. One outing was at the Santa Anita Racetrack. He was there to go over the horses of his favourite trainer, Doug. He always treated his horses first each time before he treated any other horses. Michael notes to the trainer that he is running a horse today called Milky

Way. The trainer said yes, but he has been a disappointment and not doing well. He is a claiming horse bought by an owner but wasn't doing well at all. Michael tells him he is going to go over and give this horse some special treatment. He tells the trainer, "I am going to make him feel so good when he runs this afternoon. I am going to make him run so fast he is going to run right out of his skin. Later that day, Milty Way is running in a mile and sixteenth race. He is the 2nd longest shot on the board in a ten-horse field in the morning line.

Michael goes out to be near the starting gates so he can watch the horses as they beak from the gate. Milty Way breaks from the top and goes into the first turn, leading by two lengths. Michael was not happy to see this as the horse who usually took the lead early didn't make it to the finish line first place. Milty Way is still two lengths ahead as they continue around the track. As they head down the home stretch, the announcer yells, here come the other horses to challenge Milti Way. It was like Milty heard that. Milti Way puts on a burst of speed and lengthens his lead to four lengths. The horse finishes the race in front by over six lengths, all by himself.

He is the second-longest long shot on the board. Wow, the leprechaun smiles to himself. He did run out of his skin. After the race, he walks over to see the trainer and rider. He spots them coming his way, heading towards the winners' circle. The trainer spots

Michael. He yells out, Mike, you did it; he did run right out of his skin as you said and left it all over the track he cries as he waves his arm in a big circle. He tells Michael you need to be in the winner's circle. When they are all lined up to get the picture taken, the trainer puts his arm around Michael and pulls him into the center of the picture. He points to Michael and says, here is why we are in the winner's circle. It is because of him and what he did with this horse.

He certainly had lived up again to the reputation he had earned as a Horse Whisperer and healer. The leprechaun, a ball player, had hit another Grand Slam. This is sometimes kind of hard to believe, but it is not BS. Below is a picture of the horse Michael treated. The horse went on to win two races in a row.

Over the years, Michael was able to train his own horses and heal and help horses all over the country. He was highly respected and very much in demand by horse trainers and owners at all the major tracks in California.

Michael treated hundreds of horses very successfully, to the joy and satisfaction of the trainers and owners whose horses won their races. As you saw in the picture before, he is in the winner's circle. We could fill a very thick book with pictures of Michael being in the winner's circle after having treated a horse. The one you see in the next picture is the first horse Michael treated for one of the top trainers in the world. The horse won the race in a photo finish, winning by less than a quarter inch. The horses, the owners, and the trainers loved him, and he was always in very much demand. He would probably still be doing this if his body had held up. He told me It was one of the most satisfying things that he had ever done. It is an art and skill that very few have mastered to such a high degree.

Michael said if it weren't for his stroke, he probably would still be doing it. It was such a rewarding thing to do in so many ways. Here is just one of many, many pictures of Michael being in the winners' circle after treating a horse before a big race.

 Fulfilling A Dream

In 2011, near the end of the year, Michael had a stroke at the Santa Anita racetrack in California. He ended up in the hospital for six days and almost died in the neurological trauma center. He was told by his doctor that it would be wise to give up a horse chiropractor, or he could have another stroke or heart attack and possibly die. While he was in the hospital, he thought he might not have much time left. As he lay there, he is thinking if the Lord gave him more time, what could he do with the rest of his life? He thinks maybe do some fishing and possibly become a guide or get a thoroughbred racehorse, train it himself, and win some races with it. He thought to himself, what to do first. He thinks he will probably do the horse thing first, and when he is done with that, he could then do the fishing thing for however long he may have left. Again, with the Lord's help, the leprechaun again defies the odds.

The day Michael is released from the hospital, he makes his rounds of the trainers he has treated so many horses for. He lets them know he will not be coming back as he has had a serious stroke. He will no longer be doing the horse chiropractic. The owners, of course, are sad to see him go. It was the morning he was over at the office of his favourite trainer, Doug. Michael had worked on many horses for Doug and helped his horses win many races.

Michael wanted to personally thank him for letting him treat al his horses and to let him know he wouldn't be able to service him any longer. Michael had examined and given the go-ahead on race day for almost every horse raced by this trainer. It was the first thing he did every morning. He would treat his horses first before he would go and treat any other horses.

He left Doug's office and walked through the horse barn out to the road between the stables. As he stepped out onto the road from the stable, he almost bumped into a guy walking down the road. Michael recognized him as another owner and trainer at the track. This fellow had a very poor image and reputation with Michael and with others at the track. In Michael's opinion, this trainer did not look after or properly maintain the horses in his possession and care.

This fellow tended to neglect his horses. He was quite the scoundrel. He would feed them with leftover hay. He would use stall shavings from other barns that had been peed and pooped on for his horse's stall. This gives you a snapshot of how this fellow looked after and treated his horses. Just prior to this, Michael had been musing to himself about where he would find a horse to acquire to train and race. As this fellow came abreast of Michael, the first words out of his mouth were, "Do you want to buy a racehorse?" Michael looked up and thought, "You do work quickly, Lord." This was the first and only time anyone ever made an offer to him to buy a racehorse.

Michael then thought, knowing what this character was like, I wonder what he is trying to offload on me. Michael answered in the affirmative, and they started walking over to the barn where the trainer kept his horses. As they walked, Michael asked many questions about the training methods he used. Knowing this trainer's reputation, Michael decided if he ended up buying the horse that, he would do just the opposite of what this guy was espousing. As they approached the stable where the horse was stalled, a rank odour was emanating from it. It smelled of a stall that was rarely or never cleaned.

When they finally looked into the stall, Michael observed a very sad and depressed-looking horse that was obviously very poorly cared for. Michel gritted his teeth and asked him how much he wanted for the horse. The trainer said 2500. Without hesitation, Michael said he would take her. Part of his motivation was to get this horse out from under this sad sack of an owner-trainer. The deal is made, and the trainer leaves. Michael stays behind to talk to his new horse. He talks to her quietly and tells her he is her new owner. He explains to her he is a king and has a castle, and she will be his queen, and he will be her king. He tells her she will never want for anything. She will be given everything that is befitting a queen.

He tells her she is the kind of horse who has been on the wrong side of the tracks. You are so far from the tracks you don't even know the tracks are there. He tells her that it has all now changed.

She will race and win, and he will do his best to ensure she never gets hurt. Now you know, of course, that leprechauns talk to horses. The next morning, he had her moved to a new stall with new bedding and lots of fresh food. She stayed there for about a couple of weeks.

The first thing after getting the horse, he needed to get a trainer's license. He needed to do some studying and get the necessary data and then do some tests in the barn as well as written tests, which he did. He passed all with flying colours and was quickly in possession of his thoroughbred trainer's license for California. After he had his license, he trailers up his horse and brings her to Turf Paradise in Phoenix, Arizona. He goes into the racing office to register the racing license that he had from California and was issued a racing license for Arizona. Once he has that, he then registers his horse.

As he is finishing up his paperwork, Michael hears the voice of a young man who has come into the office. He recognizes it immediately as that of a young jockey he knew from California. Michael says to him, "Hi Vinny, how is it going?" The young jockey's face lights up when he sees Michael. He tells Michael he is doing very well and getting lots of rides. He thanks Michael for having referred him to this area. Michael had met this young jockey at Holly Wood Park when he was doing his Horse Chiropractic. Vinny was just starting out and wasn't getting many rides. He asked Michael how he might get more opportunities for rides.

Michael had told him if he really wanted to become a professional jockey to get more opportunities for rides, he should go over to a track in Arizona called Turf Paradise. There, he will have many more opportunities to do so. Michael had not seen him again until he met him at the Arizona racetrack. Vinny asks Michael what he is doing there. Michael tells him he has just bought a racehorse. He is going to train and race her, starting here in Arizona. Michael tells him he has a three-part puzzle to complete. He tells him I have two parts to the puzzle: I, the trainer, the horse, but I am missing a piece, the jockey. I came over here to find you and see if you would like to be the third piece and complete the puzzle.

I need a jockey to ride my new horse and I would very much like to have you take on the job. Would you be interested in doing so? Michael tells him he would be the only rider and tells him he would have to be available to ride when Michael needs him.

The young man happily agrees, and a winning partnership is formed. The puzzle is now complete. Michael registers his new horse as Gallant Victory, and he is assigned a stall at the track. Michael surely keeps his word to his new queen. He puts at least a foot of new shavings on the floor to make it easy to stand on for the Queen. He cleans out daily the soiled material and replaces it with new ones. He fills the back of the stall with three different types of hay: Alfalfa, Bermuda, and Timothy. He told me he would pull the flakes apart and spread some of each one out so she could eat any time she wanted. She was a queen, so she ate like a queen. He makes sure she always has fresh water and feeds her a daily regimen of 14 to 16 different tasty health and wellness supplements. Most horses would only get 6 to 8. Daily, she gains muscle and stamina. Her coat starts to shine like silk. Michael takes her out daily for her exercise and takes her to the track to get her more familiar with what she will soon enough be going to race on. The other trainers and owners see how Michael is treating his horse and question him on why he is doing all that he does. Michael always answers the same way. She is the queen, and she is going to win races for me. They more or shake their heads, but it isn't long before everyone around the track knows and asks, how the Queen is doing. Michael loved to tell them all how well she was progressing. Over time, the horse muscles out into the horse she was meant to be. She is no longer looking like a lost and depressed orphan. She has a beautiful silky coat and holds herself like the regal Queen she is. Michael, when he registered her, had signed her up officially as Gallant Victory, a name she would definitely live up to. It is soon time for the horse and the new jockey to start training together. Michael walks from the barn with the young jockey astride his mount out to the entrance to the track. He then has him take the horse down the trackways, then stop and turn her sideways, facing the inner side of the track. He would then let her look around so she became more familiar with her surroundings. Each day, they would go to the track and do the same thing in the morning. It is soon apparent the horse is starting to know what this is about. This routine makes her very calm. He was giving her questions. He was doing the four-step process he used to train all the horses he had dealt with. The first day when Vinny takes her for a gallop, both he and Michael know this horse loves to run. The jockey has to hold her back as she would run full out if he had given her head to do so.

Vinny said, "Boy, this horse really wants to run. I really felt I had something beneath me." When it is time to go back to her stall, she does not want to leave the track. She wants to run some more. After several weeks of this routine, Michael decides it is time to have a look at her real potential. It was timing trial day, and she was ready to do the work. Many other horses are going to be timed on their speed that day. She is going to work three-eighths of a mile. This is the first work she has done since Michael has had her. When she was finished working, Michael asked how she did. Vinny said, "She was great. She was going smooth and fast, and I didn't even let her go, and she had a whole lot left." Michael later that day went to get a printout, and Gallant Victory had the fasted work of thirty-six horses. She had a bullet workout, which only the fasted horse gets. It is now time to test her out in an actual race. The opportunity comes soon enough. She is running a mile against eight other young horses. She goes into the gate with no hesitation. She is ready and eager to run. There are two of the other horses in this race who do not want to go in their gate and make a ruckus about it. Gallant Victory is unfazed and just stands there, ready. The gates open, and they are off, all except Gallant Victory. What happened? Well, the young jockey, being somewhat inexperienced, has not recognized fully what is going on with his mount.

The horse seemed so calm but was ready to charge out of the gate. She lunged forward very quickly and caught Vinny a little off guard. Down she goes onto her knees. Below, you can see clearly what took place. It was not a good way to start a mile race. Thankfully, Vinny remains on the horse. Michael's heart goes to his throat. Oh no, he thought.

He felt he could possibly have another heart attack when his horse went down. This was looking like it could be his first and possibly his last race with his beautiful queen. She could have damaged her ankle or knee, which would have ended her racing career right then and there. He feared the worst but hoped that she would be okay. Thankfully, Vinny does not get thrown off; the horse quickly recovers from her stumble, gets up, and gallops off in hot pursuit of the rest of the field, now many lengths in the lead. Going into the first turn, she is about twenty lengths behind the leader.

He listens to the announcer as he walks back towards the Stands. His leprechaun ears suddenly perk up. He hears the announcer say, "And here comes Gallant Victory, coming up fast. She is now in 6th place as they come around to the home stretch. She is making her move on the leaders as they come down to the wire." After falling she comes in third by less than a length.

Michael could hardly believe what he was hearing. His step quickened. He had to talk to his jockey and see the replay of the race. He thanks God and hurries on. He meets the horse and jockey as they come off the track. Vinny is looking somewhat like a hangdog as Michael comes up to them. I screwed up, are the first words out of his mouth. "It is okay," Michael tells him. "It is your first race with her, and you both seem to be all right. There will be another race, and you will win." When they arrive at her stall, Michael tells her she has done well, and there are more races to come. He has the vet come over and check her out to ensure she has not hurt herself. The vet gives her the green light.

Michael thanks God once again and gives a sigh of relief. Michael would give her a few weeks before he would race her again. Her second race is another mile-long race. Race day is once again upon them. Michael instructs his jockey one more time. "Hold her back until you get around the backstretch. Then, give her head to her and hold on." "Don't worry," Vinny says, "this is her race." Michael places himself by the fence overlooking the finish line.

The gates open, and the track announcer is heard. They're off. Vinny keeps her back as they have planned. As they go up the backstretch, he starts to let her open up. Her stride opens, and she starts to gain ground. As she comes midway on the turn for home, she is passing all the horses on the outside. She is in fifth, fourth, third, and closing on the leaders. At the top of the stretch, she takes the lead and heads home all by herself. Vinny is sure he has the race in the bag. He eases off a very little as the wire is coming up quickly. At the back of the pack, there is another horse that has been making its move and passes all the other horses. Vinny does not see the horse coming up on him as the jockey keeps his horse directly behind. Vinny couldn't see what was occurring. At that last possible moment, the other horse comes up at the wire, and they cross in a photo finish. When the results are announced, the other horse wins the race with a nose.

He can't believe it. By easing off, he has given away the race. It is a very forlorn locking jockey who meets Michael when he comes off the track. "I screwed up again," he says. "I will understand if you want a new jockey," he tells Michael. "Yes, I know, you made a mistake, he tells him, but you can't do anything about what happened. You learn from your mistakes. I told you when we started this project that you would be the jockey and the only jockey that still stands. You will be riding her when she wins. You can be sure Vinny breathed a sigh of relief. I will bring her in as a winner," he tells Michael. "I know you will," Michael replied. "This one is behind us. Let us make sure the next one is the winning one."

It was about four or five weeks later; another opportunity came to race Gallant Victory. It is another long-mile race. Michael tells Vinny to just run the same race. Hold back for the first half, then pour the coal on. Michel goes to the small bleachers in front of the grandstands, stands the race day, and sits overlooking the finish line. There is another older couple sitting there. He asked the lady who she liked in the race. She said the number 4 horse. He asked her husband what horse he liked, and he said the number six horse. The husband then asks Michael what horse he likes in the next race. Michael tells him he likes the number eight horse. The fellow asks him if he knows the horse well.

Michael tells him it is his horse that he has trained. The guy asks him if he thinks his horse will win. Michael tells him she can run a great race today. Should we bet on it to win, they ask? Michael says it is up to them, but he feels she is a winner.

They were going to place a bet, but it was too late as the race was about to start. Michael then asks them if they had ever been in the winner's circle after a horse race. No, they replied. Well, Michael tells them, if my horse wins today, you are invited. Their faces lit up.

They're off came the announcer's voice over the loudspeakers. It is another mile race with a ten-horse field. Michael watched as the Horses raced into the first turn. As they went into the first turn, Vinny was holding Gallant Victory to the back of the pack down along the rail as they had planned. Around the turn they go, and Gallant Victory is still trailing the field. As they go up the backstretch, she continues to trail. As they go into the far turn, Vinny starts to make his move with Gallant Victory. At the top of the turn, she moves into 5th place. Around the far turn, they go, and Vinnie starts to give the horse her head as she now continues to pick up her stride. Midway on the turn, she is on the outside, moving up closer to the leaders. Coming to the top of the stretch, she starts picking off the other horses and moves into 4th, then 3rd. Gallant Victory is now pouring on the coal to continue to move up on the outside, the announcer blared.

Vinny gives her the okay to open up. Down the stretch, they come. It was like she turned on the afterburners. Her stride lengthened, and it seemed her hoofs were not even touching the ground. The two leaders in front of her have been leading for the whole race. She has literally left the rest of the horses in her dust. As they are coming wire, the announcer blares out, and here comes Gallant Victory storming up on the grandstand side to challenge the leaders and goes right on by to win by three lengths. This time, Vinny let her run full out as she breezed across the finish line. "Wow, your horse did it!" the couple cried out as they turned to face Michael. "That was a wonderful race."

"Yes, indeed, it was," Michael beamed. Now, come on, let's go down to the winners' circle and congratulate the winner. The three were soon down to where the winning horse and jockey were there to be presented for having won the race. You see the picture of them all with Gallant Victory in the winner's circle.

You can tell she feels quite proud of her accomplishment. Michael has fulfilled a dream. He has purchased a sad and mistreated horse and built her back up into a beautiful racehorse. He trained her and brought her to the true though bred she is and made her into a winner.

His skills and ability as a trainer and horse whisperer showed what can be done. Over the years, Michael bred and owned many horses, quarter horses, and thoroughbreds. He won many other races with his horses, but many times, as mentioned earlier, wins were taken away from him by unscrupulous people, where greed and false pride were the order of the day. Despite the negatives involved in the industry, Michael has said that racing horses has been one of the most exciting things he has done in his life. For this leprechaun, with God watching over him, he had hit another Grand Slam. A few races later, Michael, where she also had done well, while walking her back to her stall, noticed she seemed to be slightly favouring her left front hoof.

Michael has the vet come over and have a look at it. He explains to Michael that it was a slight sprain. It should not be a major problem and will probably heal up. Michael, having had an earlier bad experience with one of his quarter horses, was not so sure.

He thought it over for a few days and then made the decision he would not take any chances of hurting his Queen. He retired her as a winner. He had accomplished his goal of acquiring and training a winning thoroughbred racehorse. He let Vinny know what he had decided and thanked him very much for helping him achieve his dream. The young jockey continued with his winning ways.

Michael was able to find a new owner for his Queen, who wanted her as a fine broodmare. Michael sold her on the condition they would not race her, and if they did, the contract would be broken. He would take her back. Michael kept her racing registration papers to ensure it. Michael has not been involved with horses to any degree since he sold his racehorse. He still has many friends in the horse business that he made over the years. Michael had also made plans to do a tour as a Horse Whisper and do seminars on how to best train one's horse. That venture, unfortunately, was shelved when his shoulder, which had been injured years ago, started to become very painful. He had to go in and have it operated on. He had to have several pins put in to stabilize it.

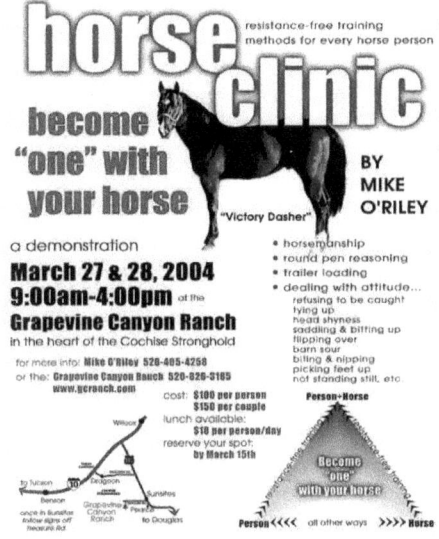

You see the photo of a brochure he had made to promote his horse clinics. Michael still has a love of horses, and it is apparent that he misses being around them. We could fill a book with the many adventures of his life with horses.

Again, if things had not occurred in Michael's life the way they did, this book would never have been written. Michael, at the very least, would be down on his ranch, training and racing horses. Michael has certainly left his mark on many horses and their trainers and owners. If he is up to it, he is looking at the possibility of putting on a couple of horse clinics and videoing them so some of his knowledge can be passed on to other horse lovers.

Now, recalling what Michael decided he wanted to do after his stroke. One was to find, train, and have a winning thoroughbred racehorse. This he accomplished with flying colours. His second idea had been to go fishing and possibly be a fishing guide. I am happy to say that although he has not become a professional guide, Michael indeed got his boat, a beautiful 19.5-foot bass boat, which he fully restored and has gone fishing in. That story is still a work in progress. Below is a picture of the boat ready to go. Michael has been very busy with his business at the Mesa market; so the fishing has taken a somewhat back seat but continues to be an ongoing story.

# Michael—Man of God

Michael, at a very young age, had never been one searching for serious spiritual endeavours. But one day, there was a knock at the door. A new pastor stopped by to introduce himself and invited us to come into the church. It was called Vista La Mesa Christian Church. His mother agreed they would come. It was a regular church. There was no Sunday school. He was given a small New Testament, which he still has today. Here is a picture of him as that young person and a picture of that New Testament, which he still has to this day. It sits near his checkout at his Mesa Market store. One Sunday, during a sermon, he heard God speak to him and say, "Someday you will be doing this." This scared Michael, and it really stuck with him his whole life.

He was raised as a Christian but did not really get seriously interested until he was in his early twenties. This was the time when he was laid up and recuperating from his serious ankle injury that occurred when he was playing basketball. Michael would sit in his easy chair at home with his whole leg up in a full-length cast.

A good part of every day, he would sit there and watch the TV. Back then, he did not have many choices of how he could spend his days. There were no remotes and only a couple of channels. It was a Sunday morning on this one channel where a preacher was espousing the gospel. His name was Oral Roberts. Michael enjoyed listening to his sermon.

After this program, immediately following, there was another show called Amazing Prophecies by a fellow named Doug Clark. He was talking about some book in the bible called Revelations. Michael did not understand this fellow and sort of dismissed him as being somewhat crazy.

Michael continued to watch both shows every Sunday. With his situation, there wasn't much choice. He was laid up and couldn't work due to his injury. There were not many options other than to watch week after week. This fellow Doug Clark would keep quoting scriptures in reference to God's prophecies and of God's End Times happening. Michael decided he was going to start keeping notes and verify what he heard by finding it out in his own bible. The following Sundays, Michael made notes of all the scriptures quoted and started looking in his own Bible. He started to understand more and more what the fellow was talking about. It was on a Sunday, several months in, and Michael was out of his cast. Doug announced he would be visiting live at various other churches in the near future. He said he would be doing a sermon in El Cajon in a few weeks. It was a church called Harvest Temple. The church just happened to be half a block down from where Michael was living.

When he found out the date Doug was going to be there, Michael told Margie that they were going to go and see him in person. The day Doug was to present, Michael and Margie headed down to the church a little early to ensure they could get a front-row seat. Before the presentation started, a man came up and introduced himself as the pastor of the church and thanked them for coming. He said he hoped they would enjoy the presentation and come back another time for a visit. Michael really loved the presentation. It was making more and more sense to him.

A couple of weeks later, while Michael was away working, a husband and wife, members of the church, paid a visit and invited them to come into the church. A couple of weeks later, while Michael was at home, the church music director visited and again invited them to come in for service. Margie then mentioned to Michael she had forgotten to tell him they had been visited and invited earlier when he was away. This time, Michael told him they would be there the next Sunday for service, which they did. They then started attending church regularly each Sunday. Michael enjoyed being there and was volunteering his help when he could and as needed.

The Pastor took Michael under his wing and tutored him on the understanding of God's word and of the possibilities of being part of the church's goings on. Michael eventually became a regular full-time member of the Church and, down the road, became an elder of the Church. He eventually became a fully ordained minister of the church. Michael became head of the youth ministry with many young people under his tutelage. One of the problems of working full-time at the church was a lack of income. He was only making 500 a month, not enough to pay all the bills and look after his family. Michael had a wife and two growing boys to look after. Michael needed a solution, so he prayed to God for help with his dilemma because he knew God would be there for him. He knew God would not leave him stuck out on a limb.

The pastor came to see him one day. He told Michael he knew that it was difficult to make a go of it financially, raising a family and paying the bills on $500 a month. He told Michael if he could find some work to make some extra money that wouldn't interfere with his church work, to go for it. Michael knew the Lord would help him as needed. He soon heard there was a new project going up in the local area. Six hundred navy housing units were being built. He heard his friend, head of the carpenters, was running the job. Michael called him up and asked if there might be work for him. Now, Michael was known for his ability to plumb and line walls of new structures like no one else could.

He told his ex-boss that he was able to work 7 am to 9 am Monday to Thursday and all-day Friday, his one day off at the Church, for a total of sixteen hours a week. Would that work? Knowing what Michael was capable of, there was a quick response, of course, and Michael was hired. Michael started the very next Monday.

He was soon making an extra 400 a week for his work. He had only been on site for a few weeks when one morning, as he was leaving, when he came up to the gate, the superintendent of the job stepped out in front. He puts his hands out for Michael to stop. He walks up to the window and asks Michael if he is working the job.

He says he has noticed him leaving at this time more than once. Michael tells him, yes, he works from 7 to 9 Monday through Thursday and all-day Fri. He tells him he works another job, which starts at 10. The super tells Michael, well, if you aren't going to work the same hours as everyone else, don't bother to come back. Michael goes back to the job site to find his boss and let him know what has gone down. He relates to him what the super has told him. His boss, who is also his friend, is not pleased, to say the least. He tells Michael, get in the truck, and I will go take care of this now.

They head over to the super's office. They go into the office, and his boss asks the super, "Did you just tell my employee not to come back if he doesn't work here all day"? The super tells him yes, he did. His boss replies, "This is my employee, he works for me." He tells the super, "I decide what hours he works. If you ever do that again, you will have no carpenters working at all. I will shut this job down."

Michael said he observed several times after he was leaving workers were checking his walls out to see if they could find something to report to the super about the shoddy work Michael did. Of course, they never found anything. God had blessed the lucky leprechaun again. He had a job that lasted several months. It allowed him to pay his bills and continue to work at the church.

The pastor came to Michael one day and told him there was a troubled youth who needed some help and guidance. He thought if he worked with Michael for a while, he might be able to help straighten him out. He knew Michael was successful in any ventures he did, so he wondered if they could set up a part-time side business. He said they could go down to Mexico and buy some leather goods, bring them back, and sell them throughout the week. There were two big resort hotels in the area, so they checked one out about renting a room and selling from there. There were a lot of tourists staying there on a regular basis. They rented a room that faced the main pool area and set up shop. It turned out to be very successful. This went on for several months. They would work so it didn't interfere with the working of the church duties. The Pastor, in the meantime, had checked out for possible store locations in a big mall not too far away. He found one that was soon coming vacant. He asked Michael if the leather store could do well in a mall. Michael told him, of course, if it was set up properly. The pastor financed it, and Michael ran it along with his wife, and was a very profitable venture. A little down the road, the pastor came to Michael and told him one of the church parishioners needed some money, about eight thousand. Could Michael get it through the store and give it to the pastor so he could help out this parishioner in need? Michael told him yes; he could make it happen. He was very pleased that he could help with this matter.

In about two weeks, he, the pastor, and the parishioner met in the pastor's office. The money was handed to the pastor, who gave it to the parishioner, who then left. The pastor asked Michael to stay as he wanted to talk to him. He reaches around behind a cabinet and pulls out a large manila envelope. He then pulls out from the envelope another document and signs it. Unbeknownst to Michael, it is the agreement he had with Michael on the leather store. He then signs it and pushes it in front of Michael. It says paid in full. Michael tells him he cannot accept it. The pastor then asks him. Do you not want me to receive any Blessings? You must accept this if you want me to be blessed. Michael then accepted, and the leprechaun had another pot of gold with the Lord's blessing.

Four years into it, the mall had a new manager who decided to change the structure of the mall in the area where Michael and some other vendors had their stores. When the lease renewals became due, the cost of the leases was quadrupled. This was purposely done to get the existing tenants to bail, which they did. Thankfully, Michael had started a very successful mobile shoe business. Michael loved working at the church. He and the pastor were very close. The pastor liked Michael so well that he gave him his original leather-bound Bible. A picture of it at the beginning of this chapter. Michael still has it and reads from it daily to this day.

Michael became the pastor's right-hand man. Because of his building skills, he did the majority of the carpentry maintenance for the church. He was a very valuable asset. The church needed a bigger space to operate. One day, the pastor took Michael to see a bowling alley close by that was closed. It was large but needed some major renovation.

The pastor asked Michael what he thought. Michael told him it was a good idea and could be renovated into a very big, nice church. The Church bought the building for a very good price, and Michael was one of the main people in charge of all the renovations, saving the church thousands in labour costs. He helped to create a beautiful new church, which the congregation still uses today. After serving successfully in the Church for some time, a nasty, deceitful, and jealous faction showed itself within some of the elders of the Church. There seemed to be some jealousy there because of his close relationship with the pastor. Unbeknownst to Michael, A few of the elders purposely set up a situation to embarrass him in front of the Pastor, which they, in fact, did. When Michael saw what they were up to and how they treated him, he decided that was it.

He left that Church and didn't look back. He never left God. Once again, you do not cross a leprechaun, especially one who serves God. It was after 30 years of marriage that Michael's wife and he split up and went their separate ways. Michael is a very loyal person, and it hit him like a ton of bricks. Being the person he is, he never suspected or saw it coming. He decided at that time that he would not be betrayed again. He would put his faith fully in God and be his faithful servant. That has continued to be his operating basis to the present moment.

Michael has told me of many instances where God has sent one of his Angels to tell him of danger. There could be very bad consequences if he didn't heed the warning he was being given. The example at the beginning of the book where he was told to get up and go to the hospital now. There were many times when he was driving and told to get off the highway, which he always did. A tire would almost immediately blow or go flat. The two times he was kicked by a horse and could have easily lost his life. The time he twisted his ankle, but it was saved and where he really started to listen. The time he could have lost it on his bicycle. The times he fell off or through a roof. These are all times Michael knows his life was spared. The time he blacked out after a five thousand-mile long and tiring trip. This is another story not mentioned earlier.

A very interesting thing happened with Michael. I bring this up to show that there is a very strong spiritual side to Michael with which he is strongly connected. He was still living in the San Diego area with his wife and his boys. He had just bought a brand-new Ford truck. He also bought a new boat and trailer. He had special new wheels put on the truck just before they left on their trip.

He decided to take the family on a fishing trip up to Lake Cachuma, about three hundred miles north in central California near Santa Barbara. To get there, he had to drive up the coastal highway north of Santa Barbara, then go east inland, then up and over the mountains to reach the lake. Michael really didn't notice anything out of the ordinary until he started down the back side of the mountains. The trip down was very steep and fast on the final stretch, which ended at the foot of the mountains.

Michael would feel a slight intermittent sway at times and put it down to the fact of towing the boat behind or wind blowing off the mountain. He asked Margie if she noticed, and she said she did but didn't feel anything dangerous. At the bottom, there was a turn-off leading into the campground onto a gravelled road that veered off to the right. Michael slowed and turned off the main road. He had no sooner cleared the main highway with a truck and trailer when there was a large bang.

The back end of his truck went down with a crash, his back left wheel bounced past him down the road, and the trailer dug into the gravel road. There was damage done to the front of the trailer, the tongue was bent, and the back left rear of the truck. After three hundred-plus miles, the back left wheel came off, and all aboard were safe. Michael knew that if that wheel had come off at any other time, especially coming down the steep mountain road, there was a high likelihood all would not have ended well. Michael and his family stopped to pray and thanked God for saving their lives. His Angels, along with his leprechaun luck, had saved him again. There is very much so a greater power, alive and well, in Michael's life.

In 2017, Michael decided he was going to go rafting on the Salt River in Arizona. The river is tame in the summer as the water flow is down. There are some slightly deeper areas and some mildly turbulent areas where the water is shallow. Even though it appears very serene and tranquil, one still needs to be cautious. It is a beautiful sunny summer morning, and there are hundreds of people doing the same thing. Michael is sitting on a big inner tube bobbing down the river like many others. He has a smaller tube to hold some drinking water, plus he holds his valuables like his wallet with about $500 in it. The length of the route most people take is several miles long. Well, Michael is enjoying his ride. He gets to the point where everyone finishes and gets off. He is on the far side of the river when he realizes it. He quickly clambers off his ride. Unfortunately for him, the water is a little deeper at this point. His feet do not hit the bottom. His ride slips out of his hands and goes bobbing along out of his reach, heading downstream with all his important papers. His current is strong, and Michael can't hold his position as he has nothing to brace himself against.

He loses his balance and goes tumbling down the stream. He is bouncing against the rocks under the water, and he fears for the worst. He gets his head above water to gasp for a breath of air; then down, he goes again. Fortunately for Michael, his Angels were looking out for him, and he was spotted from the shore. A strong young man wades out chest-deep, catches Michael, and brings him to a stop. He manages to brace himself well enough to keep them both in one spot, but he is unable to drag him to shore because of the strong current. He calls to get someone to come and help, and his call is answered.

Another young man comes out, and between the two of them, they manage to get Michael safely to dry land. Michael is so weak he can't even stand. Michael thanks God for sending out the two strong men to save him and get to live another day. Do you believe it? Another brush with death, but again, this leprechaun lives to tell the tale another day.

In 2020, just before the national election, a very profound experience occurred with Michael. He had just sat down waiting for the election results, expecting to hear Trump won. Instead, he hears a voice say, "Biden is going to win the election," and then proceeds to tell him why he was going to win. He is told to go and get a pen and paper and write down what he is told.

Michael knew that it was God and his holy spirit speaking to him. He quickly went and retrieved paper and pen. He then transcribed what he was being told.

As history has shown, even though it was done through cheating, Biden became President.

Now, to interject again, this is not the first time God has spoken to Michael directly. Several times while driving, he would hear the voice tell him to get off the highway immediately. Michael always listened, and when he did get off the highway, a tire would blow out, one that could have caused a major accident if he had been driving at full highway speed when it happened. The other one that saved his life was the one we described at the beginning of the book when he almost died of an allergic reaction to a medication he was taking. God told Michael he needed his help to let the people know that end times were soon to be coming and that they needed to be warned to take appropriate actions. Michael continued to receive more and more information from God and soon had pages and pages of notes. He asked me if I could help type it up and put it in a format that he could present to Pastors of different official Church Congregations to give out to them. This was done. Michael has continued to do so. He had special signs made up and put on his car. He also had a special two-sided A-frame board sign made up, which he has been putting out daily in various locations to get the word out. Michael certainly walks the talk in his everyday activities.

We put up a new website called comingtimes.org and created an FB page for him as well to get the message out to as many people as possible. He is a true servant of God. Although he is not totally certain why he was chosen, he feels it is because he made the decision to have this close relationship with his creator. He continues to promote what he has been told and will continue to do so unless he is informed otherwise. Michael has been saved from the jaws of death so many times by his personal relationship with God that he has total certainty about the message that has been given to him to pass on to the world.

 # Some Final Thoughts

Now, originally, when we started this book, it looked like it could be a very voluminous series of stories that this leprechaun had to tell. It certainly could have been. Michael has lived and been successful in so many areas of life we felt it would be more appropriate to tell some of his more memorable ones and give the reader the flavour of this leprechaun. His stories are all good and definitely make for interesting reading. On reflecting and seeing what has been written this far, we decided it would be better to keep them limited to shorter versions. We could always do a follow-up at some possible future time. He has many more entertaining tales to impart from his life of close to 80 years. We could do a whole book on his stories with his experiences in the horse industry alone. I believe what has been written here gives the flavour of the individual, his successes and his failures, and how he has overcome adversities and turned the tide to bring off successes where other men have given up.

He has survived more than his fair share of near-death experiences where the stories could have ended, but yet here he is, still telling his tales. It has been a pleasure writing them down and making them available for you. It is truly hoped you will enjoy reading them. We look forward to the possibility of bringing you more adventures of Michael along with some antidotes you find useful and maybe improve situations in your life. Now that you have read these tales, do you possibly believe in leprechauns? Whether you do or you don't or just may suspect, just do not cross one, or you might not like the results you get. We wish Lucky four leaf clovers for you. May the luck of the leprechaun be with you, and may you find your own pot of gold. May God bless you for allowing me to be a leprechaun and tell you my stories.

Below is Michael's card he had made up. On the card, he has part of a scripture that explains to him how and why he has been saved and blessed so many times in his life. This has always been one of his favourite scriptures. Psalms 91:11 For he shall give Angels charged over watching thee to keep thee in all thy ways. No matter what Michael has done or what has occurred in his life, he has always been aware of his Special Messengers who have been watching over him and helping him to be safe. Although he may or not be a full-fledged leprechaun, he can state with certainty that those watching over him do exist and have been a major part of his life and his relationship with God.

Dedicated to my brother, Donald Oliver O'Riley

My brother Don passed away on July 17th, 2022, just a couple of months short of his 80th birthday.

Don has been my best friend since we were very young brothers. As you will read in this book, we were involved in many adventures together, from having our own landscape maintenance business as kids, playing many types of sports together, and running several different restaurant venues, we have always been very close. He was just a year and a half older than me, and we were both very competitive.

Don was over six feet tall while I was quite a bit shorter; being a leprechaun, we are prone to being smaller in stature. I made up for my lack of size by being more aggressive, which opened the playing field. I branched out into many new and different entrepreneur activities, and my brother stayed working within the restaurant field, which he was very good at. In my younger years, he was very instrumental in getting me involved in that field as well. I really appreciate him for being a guiding influence in my life. Although I miss his presence in the flesh, I know I will be with him again down the road.

www.ingramcontent.com/pod-product-compliance
Lightning Source LLC
Chambersburg PA
CBHW041316110526
44591CB00021B/2798